24.N
3
13.
30 JAN
24. A
26.J
31. OCT
12. DEC
26 F
28

MATCH FISHING TACKLE AND BAITS

Other books by the same author

MATCH ANGLING

COARSE FISHING

TO MY YOUNGER DAUGHTER KATE

Last-minute tackle (*by courtesy of Angling Telegraph*)

Match Fishing Tackle and Baits

Bill Bartles

Adam & Charles Black, London

First published 1975
by A. & C. Black Ltd.
4, 5 and 6 Soho Square London W1V 6AD

© 1975 Bill Bartles

ISBN 0 7136 1513 3

reproduced, stored in a retrieval system, or transmitted in
any form or by any means, electronic, mechanical,
photocopying, recording or otherwise, without prior
permission of A. & C. Black Ltd.

Filmset and printed in Great Britain by
BAS Printers Limited, Wallop, Hampshire

CONTENTS

DRAWINGS IN THE TEXT

PHOTOGRAPHS

INTRODUCTION

Nobody would deny that luck – or the lack of it – can play a big part in our world of angling. And in match fishing especially, it is a good thing that top experts in one part of a river will often be struggling to tempt few and far-between fish while some comparative novice further along will do a lot of things wrong, lose a number of 'netters', and then put enough on the scales for top prize.

By the law of averages, though, the real expert is more likely to fill nets and show a profit over a period of a few seasons. He will sometimes make his own luck, and given one of, say, ten or twenty potentially winning pegs in a match length, he will exploit his swim to the full and catch those extra fish that are to separate him from the runners-up.

Most important of all, the top match angler will rarely be caught napping as regards equipment. It is so easy to be wise after the event, but every matchman should aim to be well informed about the venue and start off with the most likely winning tackle rig and baits.

The latest trend is for match anglers to study the recent form of a match water, decide whether big or small fish will offer best chance of success, and then go all out for either chub, barbel and bream, roach and dace, or even tiny fish like bleak and gudgeon. This is in complete contrast to the anglers of a few decades ago who simply fished for anything that came along.

Obviously, altogether different baits and tackle rigs are required for various species. And in this complementary book to my earlier one *Match Angling*, I am describing all the essential tackle you will need to catch a winning net of a few hundred 'tiddlers' or a number of 2, 3 and 4-pounders. I am also dealing with a variety of winning baits, ranging from big juicy lobworms down to the tiny bloodworm.

Every season there are men who fail to cash in on, or even realise that they have drawn, a good swim, and it is my aim in this book to help you choose the right tackle and baits, and not be one of the many who have one long run of 'bad luck'. Never forget, you get prizes and pound notes for winning not losing, and that, after all, is what match angling is all about.

BILL BARTLES

Part One

TACKLE

Assuming that you have already been bitten by the match fishing bug and have decided to fish for cups, medals and money in a big way, my first advice is that you should get the best tackle you can afford right at the beginning. The biggest mistake – if you are aiming for the top in our sport – is to make a start with cheap, inferior rods and reels, and then have to go out a year or so later and invest some more money on quality tackle.

Ideally, in your first year of match angling you should be reasonably well equipped to catch fish quickly from the waters where you are competing. If, for instance, you are to do all your early match fishing on a mainly-roach river like the Trent, you could cut initial costs by delaying the purchase of a swingtip rod, Arlesey bombs and things like target boards. On the other hand, you should be looking for a long, light rod and a selection of well-made floats.

Of course, if your early contests are likely to be on sluggish, wide fenland-type drains where bream anglers dominate the prize lists, by all means concentrate on tackle to suit that species. As time goes by – perhaps collecting a few cups and a little money on the way – you will eventually widen your horizons, and at this stage you should be equipped with various rods, floats and other things to enable you to catch bream from the River Welland, roach from the Trent, and barbel from the Yorkshire Ouse.

When buying match tackle, be it an expensive rod, a reel, or merely a few spade-end hooks, I strongly advise you to go to a proper tackle dealer, one who fishes himself, and preferably one who competes in top-flight matches. If you go into a toy shop which sells bits and bobs of fishing tackle, you cannot expect a non-angling assistant to understand the differences between stick floats and antennas, or even a swan shot and an AAA. In any case, many fishing tackle shops run by enthusiasts are regarded as a sort of club house, a place where fishy pictures and perhaps glass-cased fish hang on the walls, and fishing days are relived. If you ask a match angler-cum-tackle dealer for soft shot that is not too deeply cut, he will know why.

As far as things like rods and floats are concerned, it often pays to make your own. Besides costing considerably less, you can fashion them to suit your particular requirements. Don't worry if your finished rod or float is not as shiny as some of those mass-produced ones in the shops. The gloss on a rod is to catch you, and it is actually against the angler who is trying to tempt shy fish.

As each match season comes and goes we all tend to amass a bigger-than-ever collection of tackle, and it is a well-known fact that no matter how big a basket you get, it nearly always ends up crammed to the lid. The best plan at the end of each season is to discard anything that has not been, and is not likely to be, used. Otherwise you can end up loaded like a packhorse and not in any fit state to fish when you reach your peg, especially after a long walk along a river like the Severn. With more and more match anglers becoming car owners, the problem of tackle weight is, however, no problem at all on a number of big-match waters. From Kirkstead to Dogdyke on the River Witham you can drive right up to your peg number, and it is the same on the North Bank stretch of the Nene near Peterborough, and the Ten Mile Bank to Denver Sluice reaches of the Great Ouse. Certainly you may not need all the tackle described in the following chapters, but it is equally certain that you will have to be adequately equipped for the species or waters on which you are going to specialise.

1 RODS

Gone are the days when matchmen could only have one set of tackle rigged up on the river bank. Perhaps following the example set by the continentals, particularly the French, Belgians and Italians who often have a vast array of ready-for-action tackles propped up behind them, the N.F.A. (National Federation of Anglers) brought their match rules up to date, and now allow each competitor to have any number of rods and tackles assembled behind him. This has brought a big transformation to the match scene, and whereas competitors were loath to change tactics because it meant one set of tackle had to be stripped down before another was rigged, match anglers today are more versatile and are frequently changing from one rod to another during a match. This amendment to match rules has been particularly welcomed by men who regularly compete on bream rivers such as the Witham, Welland and Nene. One minute they may be trying with swingtip or quiver-tip tackle for far-off bream, and the next few casts can be with float tackle just over the near-side weed fringe.

In an effort to cut tackle costs to a minimum, you may be tempted to go out and buy one of those so-called combination rods. Ideally, these have various interchangeable sections which, when permutated, should give you a choice of weapons for various types of fishing. In reality, however, each particular combination is a compromise, with the float rod, quiver-tip and swingtip set-ups rarely being just right.

Whatever type of rod you are buying or making, the first essential is that it should be light, and certainly not too heavy to hold in your hand for five or six hours. Fortunately, advancements in the production of hollow fibre-glass blanks have made it easier to produce ultra-light match rods. In the old days of tonkin cane and built cane tops, an average of one ounce per foot in length was difficult to attain. And yet today, the 12-footers in thin-walled hollow glass go as low as 7 ounces, complete with rings and winch fittings. You can get a 13 foot rod weighing less than 9 ounces, while there are 14 foot versions in glass going to around 10 ounces. These days, ferrules are usually built in to the fibre-glass blanks, avoiding the need for separate pairs made of metal. Unfortunately as rods become lighter, they also become more prone to damage, particularly when being packed into small motor cars or left lying on a river bank where spectators or 'non-catchers' are wandering about. However, should you have the misfortune to have some clumsy soul put a size 12 wellington boot onto your winning rod, I shall be giving advice on do-it-yourself rod repair later in this chapter.

Apart from being as light as possible for the job it has to perform, there are other important things I look for in a match rod. The end runner (or rod ring as they are alternatively known) on the top section must have a good quality 'jewel' insert such as Cintox. Also desirable is a 'jewelled' runner on the butt of the rod, the nearest one to the reel. As important as quality rod rings is the diameter of the cork butt. The thicker it is, the more

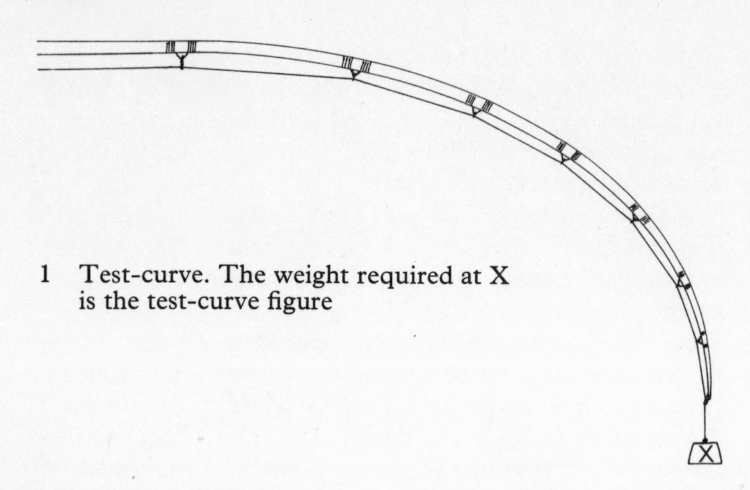

1 Test-curve. The weight required at X is the test-curve figure

difficult tackle control becomes. Some rod butts are made up of sheet cork, while others are built with cork bungs. The use of either method makes little difference on mass-produced rods, providing the diameter is small.

Many newcomers to match fishing, or any other sort of fishing come to that, are a little bewildered when they read of a particular rod having a test-curve of, for instance, 1 lb, 2 lb or even 3 lb. There is nothing complicated about it really. Simply fasten a spring balance to the top runner of the rod and then – with the rod held horizontally – pull down on the scales until the top section is bent over to about a quarter circle. The figure on the scales is the so-called test-curve of that particular rod. In complete contrast to pike rods which sometimes have test-curves of 2 and $2\frac{1}{2}$ lb, our match rods average around $\frac{3}{4}$ lb. There are light roach rods with a figure of $\frac{1}{2}$ lb, while occasionally a rod nearing 1 lb test-curve is used for pushing a big float across a wide match river. Test-curve figures are not the be-all and end-all, but it would be wrong to use a strong line and a really sloppy rod, and it would be even worse the other way round. Use a stiffish rod and a weak line, and you will be in real trouble with lost fish and broken terminal tackle. Generally speaking, a rod with a test-curve of $\frac{3}{4}$ lb will be about right for a line of 3 or 4 lb breaking strain.

While strong rods coupled with weak lines do lead to trouble, the quickest way to ruin a fishing line is continually to pull it through worn rod rings. Grooving inside rod rings is pretty common. It is caused by the line, and then in turn it reduces the diameter and breaking strain of the line.

Float-fishing rods fall mainly into two categories; those for trotting down fairly close in and snatching small fish like bleak on the surface or 'on the drop', and those stronger more-powerful versions which are used for casting heavy float rigs well across. The latter type of rod is also ideal for rod-end legering at waters like the Yorkshire Ouse and River Severn for chub and barbel.

Dealing first with those super-lightweight weapons for rod-end roach and bleak etc., they mostly range between 11 and 12 feet in length, with ones of 13 feet occasionally brought into action. A good idea is to buy a set of fibreglass blanks such as those that go under the brand name of LERC, and complete it at home. Actually, with a set of blanks with built-in ferrules, all you need to do is put on about eight rod rings (including the jewelled ones at butt and tip), waterproof the whippings, and cover the end 2 feet of the butt section with plastic adhesive tape. After winding the tape on spiral-fashion, all you need then is a pair of strong rubber bands to hold the reel in place. In cold weather, this plastic-taped-butt idea together with rubber bands is a lot warmer to the fingers than metal winch fittings.

Whether you buy your rods or make them, I strongly advise you to butt-load them with lead, especially those reserved for high-speed roach and bleak fishing. There is nothing complicated about this butt-loading method of mine, you simply remove the butt cap or rubber button on the bottom end of the rod, then glue about 2 ounces of lead into the bottom of the rod butt. It is a simple job, but with 2 ounces of lead in the butt, the whole rod will be better balanced and will actually feel ounces lighter!

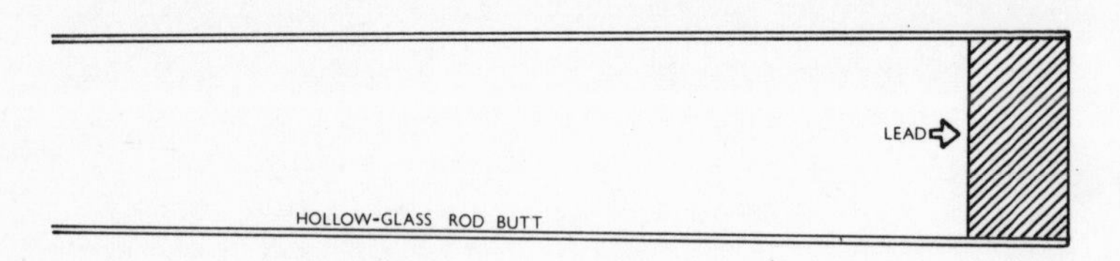

2 Butt loading method

Moving higher up the range on to those more-powerful rods that are to be used for casting heavy floats, or for rod-end legering for big fish, you should be looking for a 12 or 13-footer that has a more all-through action, is strong enough to stand the strain, yet at the same time is reasonably easy to handle. There are all-fibre-glass models on the market which are completely adequate for this far-off float fishing, but my favourite for this style is made of varying sections of hollow fibre-glass and aircraft alloy. It is produced by swingtip inventor Jack Clayton of Boston, and not surprisingly it is known as the 'Fibralloy'. Having discussed the more usual float rods that can be seen in action each weekend on rivers like the Trent and Severn, we move on now to take a look at swingtip rods, quiver-tips, roach poles and the best and only efficient way to repair a broken section of fibre-glass rod.

SWINGTIP

For matches on waters like the Huntspill River in Somerset, the Witham and Welland in Lincolnshire, and the Littleport to Denver reaches of the Great Ouse, no competition angler can afford to be without a swingtip rod. On wide, still or slow-moving waters especially, the 'tip' is time and time again a winner when big bream shoals are likely to be encountered. The funny thing is, while swingtipping produces some of our biggest match nets each season, it is one of the easiest methods when you have the right tackle and have learnt the basics of this type of legering. As swingtips are mostly used on predominantly-bream waters – where luck of the draw is probably more vital than on any other type – it isn't surprising that we hear so much of 'swingtip bingo'. This is true to a certain extent, and while some men become more proficient than others with this far-off method, there are comparative newcomers who have gone to bream waters and won against fairly stiff opposition. Swingtipping on average is a more simple affair than most types of float fishing, and this is just one reason why it is so often a winner.

As with most other things, it is better to start off with the right ideas and proper tackle from the word go. Over the years, for instance, it has been proved that a swingtip rod of between 9 and 10 feet in length is about right on most days, especially where there is some weed growth along the edges of the water. Certainly I would recommend you not even to consider any swingtip rod less than 8 feet. In fact, given a peg where the weed fringe extends well out, a weapon of 11 or even 12 feet could give you a distinct advantage. To overcome the weed fringe problem, some swingtippers with short rods often resort to standing well out into the water, but I would remind you that – in most areas of the country – the match rules do not permit 'paddling' under any circumstances.

Having decided on a length of 9, 10 or 11 feet or so to suit the type of water where most of your match fishing with swingtip is to take place, the next step is to look for a rod with quite a bit of 'give' down the middle. A lot of your swingtipping may be done with hook-length breaking strains of only 1½ and 2 lb, perhaps less, and you must have a fairly soft rod to reduce the chance of breaking off on the strike. Remember, in float fishing the line from rod tip to hook is rarely in a straight line, but when swingtipping you are often striking directly to the fish. Apart from a bit of stretch in the nylon line, a bending rod is your only way to prevent tackle and fish losses. In theory, of course, the slipping clutch should take care of any sudden shocks, but the slipping clutches on many reels leave much to be desired.

When Boston's Jack Clayton first invented the swingtip in 1959, his way with the actual tip itself was to use a piece of solid nylon, just over 12 inches in length and ⅛ inch in diameter, tapering down much thinner where it was fastened on to the rod tip. Even to this day the solid nylon idea is being used by top-class matchmen, often to good effect. These days, the tip itself is often much shorter than Clayton's prototype, and some are fitted with a screw adaptor so that they can be used on any rod you wish. To fit a detachable swingtip, the rod must have a threaded end ring, but in a matter of seconds, an orthodox general-purpose or roach rod can be rigged with a 'wiggly bit on the end' ready for catching far-off bream on leger. You can have a selection of detachable swingtips, varying in weight, and use them for different amounts of flow. On a slow-running river, for instance, you would obviously need a heavier swingtip than on, say, a stillwater canal or

A bream on swingtip from the River Witham

reservoir. No matter what type of swingtip you choose, this principle of weight to suit flow must be applied. On a rod with a permanently whipped-on tip, the only way to overcome flow problems is to add lead wire. However, if a river is flowing strongly enough to call for much weighting of the tip itself, I would dispense with the swingtip altogether and switch over to quiver-tip tactics. More about quiver-tips, though, later.

To avoid the problem of adding or taking off lead wire as the river runs stronger or slows down, inventor Clayton has more recently devised what he calls a 'cantilever' swingtip. On it is a sliding nylon collar which can be adjusted to suit any river condition the match angler is likely to encounter. While I have not yet had time to form any firm opinions on this new idea, others are already convinced it will be a winner on days when rivers like the Great Ouse and Witham are rushing out to sea.

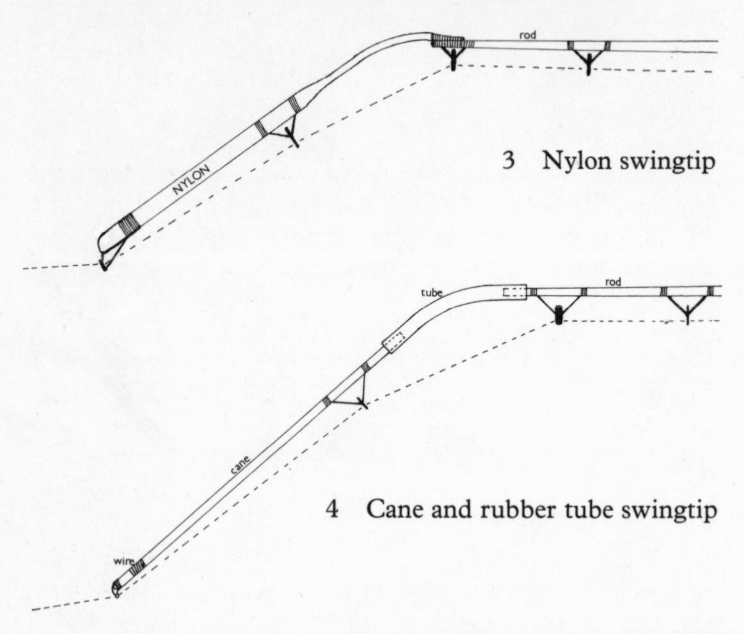

3 Nylon swingtip

4 Cane and rubber tube swingtip

In complete contrast to those who prefer all-nylon swingtips, I make mine of cane, and attach it to the rod tip with a 2 inch piece of rubber tubing. The cane is simply a 9 inch length, $\frac{1}{8}$ inch in diameter, like that you can buy in some tackle shops for making floats. The cane is fitted with a small end runner (you can make it out of a small safety pin) and an intermediate runner towards the other end. Push the rubber tube over the rod tip, join on the cane tip and you are ready for business. I carry three different-weight cane swingtips, loaded with varying amounts of fuse wire. The lighter of the three is in fact not loaded at all and is simply a piece of cane fitted with the two small rings. On those weighted with wire, it is best to whip over with silk to cover any sharp edges. Whichever type of swingtip you plump for – cane, nylon or anything else – the end ring on the rod must be of the hard-wearing jewelled type, otherwise grooving at the point of line pressure will quickly occur. As I have pointed out, heavily-weighted swingtips are not the answer to most of our fast water bite-detection problems. Quiver-tips are, though, and we can now move on to them.

QUIVER-TIP

For a number of years it has been proved that when bream waters were running pretty fast, a quiver-tip would give you a decided advantage. And then there were wins by anglers using this method when there wasn't any appreciable flow. In the 1973 First Division National Championships on the River Witham in Lincolnshire, for example, Leicester match ace Dave Downs didn't win, but he used a quiver-tip to come second with 41 lb 6 oz, not far behind winner Alan Wright who weighed in with 41 lb 10½ oz. On that fishy September day, the Witham did not run, but a point was proved and many former critics of the quiver-tip method were beginning to have second thoughts.

Generally, however, the quiver-tip is most valuable when bream are the quarry and rivers are in a hurry. In winter, especially, this relatively new idea is a vital weapon in your match fishing armoury.

Mainly, quiver-tips fall into three categories: short straight ones, short tapered ones, and longer tapered ones. Most of them are made of solid fibre-glass or similar material.

Dealing first with the short non-tapered quiver-tip, mine is a proprietary one, 15 inches long, $\frac{1}{16}$ inch diameter, and made of fibre-glass. When purchased, it was simply a piece of glass with a threaded adaptor at one end, a small ring fastened on at the other, and another fairly small rod ring about halfway along. For really sluggish waters such as fenland-type drains in summer, I found this type worked quite well. On the other hand, I was looking for an alternative to the lead wire and swingtip plan on deep-flowing rivers, especially in autumn and winter when extra water was coming in after heavy rain. To add more power to the non-tapered quiver-tip and prevent it being bent right over under a modest strain, I added another runner about 3 inches away from the adaptor. To stiffen it further at this 3-inch weak spot, I whipped the fibre-glass with silk thread. When this original type of quiver-tip first came on the market, some other match anglers found that the fibre-glass had a weak spot near to where it was fastened to the threaded adaptor. Some quiver-tips actually did break, but thanks to the silk whipping and extra runner, mine has stood the test of many match seasons.

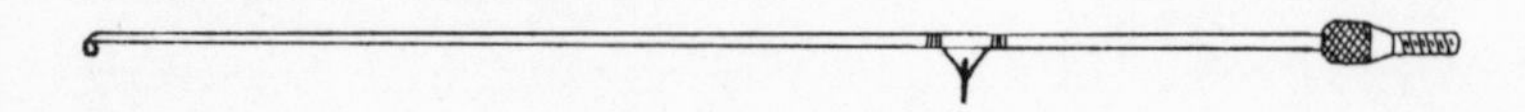

5 Tapered quiver-tip

More recently, the mass-produced quiver-tips coming into the tackle shops have been tapered types, between 15 and 18 inches in length, and like those non-tapered ones, fitted with a threaded adaptor. While I have no reason to complain of my original pattern with silk whipping, I welcome the latest tapered quiver-tips and consider them a boon to all bream anglers in search of better bite detection. A tip here for protection of a quiver-tip when it is not in use on the rod – drop it into the butt section of the rod out of harm's way. This idea, by the way, can be used for those extra-long floats that are too big to fit into a normal tackle box. Another way with detachable quiver-tips and long floats is to carry them around inside your big fishing umbrella.

Even more recently, complete top sections of rods with built-in quiver-tip are coming on to the market. Some of these have up to 24 inches of solid fibre-glass, tapering down to about $\frac{1}{16}$ inch at the very tip. For a number of years, some anglers in the York and Leeds areas have been experimenting with these extra-long quiver-tips built into top sections. Until now, they have mostly been used on the fairly fast-flowing chub and barbel rivers of Yorkshire, and to a lesser extent, on the middle reaches of the Severn. There is every reason, though, to expect the long quiver-tip fashion to spread to matchwaters such as the Great Ouse and Nene, especially when these rivers are carrying a foot or so of 'extra'.

Whichever type of quiver-tip is your final choice, it will certainly prove far more effective than a swingtip when there is a strong pull on the water. All too often, I have seen men sitting for five hours or so with a swingtip straightened out into the river. Under these circumstances, a bent rod would be the only clue that a fish is on the end of the line. It is much better to use a quiver-tip, especially if it is on a rod that is not too soft down the middle. By using a fairly pliable quiver-tip on a stiffish rod, bites are soon recognised. To be effective at all, however, the quiver-tip rod should be almost parallel with the bank on sluggish waters, and pointing straight out on fast flows such as those you are likely to find on Yorkshire rivers, the Severn, and some parts of the Thames. Point the quiver-tip straight down the line, and it is certain that you will never know if a fish grabs the bait – unless of course it pulls the rod out of your hand!

Finally, on quiver-tips, I advise you to paint some marks on the tip itself. Given a good peg with the fish feeding, bites are almost sure to come, and it is up to you to make sure you can see them clearly. I paint mine in black and white, and I can spot the slightest 'knock', no matter whether the background is water, a weedy fringe, or an intruding swan.

ROACH POLES

While the Midlands and North may take some pride in the fact that they can boast the most match anglers – but I'm not getting involved in the controversy as to whether they can boast the best – it is the Southern anglers who have been the first to realise the potential of the 'pole' on waters where men fish for money, medals and cups. The funny thing is, the long-pole idea was fairly popular in our grandfathers' day, but it went out of fashion as reels were improved and became more sophisticated. The main reason for the comeback is the new match rule which – in most parts of the country – allows you to have more than one tackle rig ready for use. With orthodox rod and reel, you simply lengthen or shorten your cast whenever it is apparent that the fish have moved out into mid-stream or come nearer in. With pole fishing, however, some sort of length selection is an absolute necessity. Also influential on the pole revolution has been the example set by some of the continentals. Faced with opposition from France, Belgium and Italy, who could catch up to 200 or so fish an hour on a pole, English world championship anglers – with rod and reel – have time and time again been left trailing. Already pole sales are starting to boom in this country, and after news of a few roach pole wins on, say, the Witham, Severn or Trent, these long tight-line weapons would be harder to get hold of than a score of lobworms on a frosty January morning.

The main asset of a pole, of course, is that you can trot a float straight downstream, even well out from the bank in difficult wind conditions. Under similar circumstances with a relatively short rod and reel, the match angler often has to sink line between rod and float, and even then there may be too much slack. Yes, the roach pole is going to come back with a real bang, especially on waters where midstream float tactics are likely to bring rich reward. New trends and ways with tackle are usually slow to gain momentum even in our competitive side of angling. Nevertheless, there are exceptions, as will be proved when more and more matchmen jump on the pole bandwagon at venues where this method is likely to be a winner.

With, say, swingtip rods, and others for rod-reel-and-float fishing at places like the Trent, one could suggest an ideal length. But the pole enthusiast is more versatile and may change rods and take off or put on sections several times during the course of a few hours. Daring to suggest an average weapon that could bring lucrative results on a number of different waters, it would, I think, be best to start off with a pole of 15 to 18 feet. I have tried and caught fish on an 18 foot version, but despite the improved materials, they are quite heavy and I certainly would not recommend a pole newcomer to be too optimistic and start off with something over 20 feet in length.

The biggest advantage with the pole is that you are able to present the bait properly. And with less slack line to bother about, there is also a better chance of driving the hook home. To avoid sudden shocks on the line and safeguard the fine tackle which is often used, the continentals frequently fasten up to a foot of high-quality elastic on the pole end, to which is fastened the nylon line. This shock-absorber idea is already being copied on this side of the English Channel. Like many other matchmen over here, I'm still learning with the pole, but I'm convinced already that my butt-loading idea, as mentioned earlier, makes for less arm aching, especially for the less-brawny ones like myself. Take it or leave it, then, that is the pole. It won't always be a winner, but it is going to be a winner much more often than it has been.

FIBRE-GLASS REPAIR

As match anglers call for lighter rods, who can blame the manufacturers who meet these needs and demands with frail ultra-light fibre-glass blanks. In an effort to cut fractions of ounces off each rod section, fibre-glass walls have become thinner and thinner, and there are those which are little thicker than stiff paper. Nevertheless, on a match rod I have never had a glass section break in two while actually fishing. In fact, I have never seen any other angler's rod break in half while a fish was on the end of the line. It is clumsy anglers, not big fish, who break rods, but it will always happen from time to time.

I have had more than my share of broken fibre-glass rods, but thanks to a repair technique that I'm going to describe, they are all back in action and as good as ever. The first rod I broke was one of the most expensive in my collection, and I must admit that my heart sank right to the soles of my wellington boots when it happened. I was moving into another swim on a match practice session, I trod on a large piece of stone, I fell down, and without even thinking, I stuck out my hand to cushion the fall. The trouble was, in that hand was the precious rod, and I'll leave you to guess what happened and what was said.

Luckily, a tackle dealer-cum-rod repairer friend of mine came to the rescue and showed me how to overcome the problem. From what he told me, it seems more and more match anglers are falling or treading on expensive rods these days. It also seems likely that many of those three-piece rods are still in four sections, propped in the corner of an outhouse or garage, and will never cast a float or leger again.

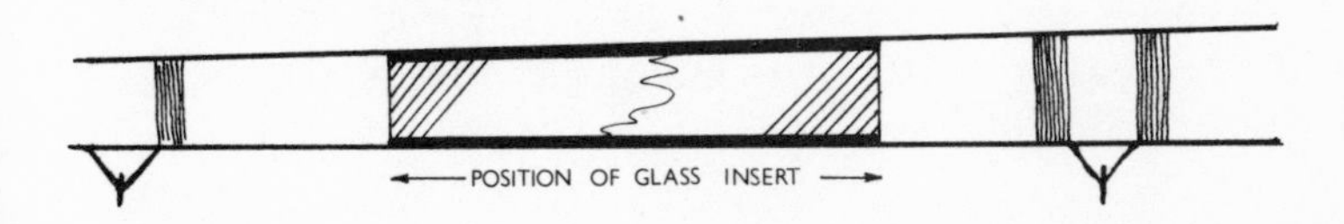

6 Fibre-glass rod repair

Anyway, here is the rod repair method I use for modern fibre-glass. Assuming that the rod section is in two halves with the ends all splintered and cracked, first of all get hold of a short section of spare hollow fibre-glass. Usually a piece of about 6 inches long will be ample, and I prefer it to be fairly thick-walled and strong. The idea is to insert the short section of glass inside the broken rod, half of it each side of the break. Obviously, you have to find a piece of glass which is the right size in diameter, and roughly the same taper as the broken rod. The next move is to glue the 6 inch section (or less, according to the amount of splintering) inside the broken rod. The best way, if possible, is to slide the glue-covered insert right up from the wide end of the broken rod section.

Otherwise, use an insert a little smaller in diameter and perhaps file a little glass from the wide end. In the latter case, more cement than usual would be needed.

Most important is the glue or bonding material. For all my rod repairs these days I use Araldite, a high-stress adhesive epoxy resin. I have had more than one break in fibre-glass – but never twice on the same rod. With this type of adhesive, you first have to mix two ingredients. I usually use a little more of the hardener than usual, and allow at least four or five days for the repair really to set. As an extra precaution, I whip over the broken piece with silk thread before the Araldite starts to harden. If the repair is on the top section of a long rod, it will feel a little heavier, but if it is along the butt, you will never notice the difference.

2 REELS

Basically, there are three types of reel for the man who fishes in contests for species such as roach, bream, chub and gudgeon – centre-pin, open-faced fixed-spool, and the closed-face. When buying a reel for match fishing, ignore multipliers and one-handled fly reels, they're certainly not for you. Mind you, within the three useful types of match reels, there are plenty of models to choose from. In fact if a newcomer browses round one of our up-to-date well-stocked tackle shops, he can be excused for being bewildered by the vast array. Here, of course, is where an experienced tackle dealer-cum-match expert can give a helping hand. A wise dealer knows that if he sells you a reel that helps to put you in the prize money, you are likely to come back week after week to stock up with groundbait, maggots, or other things. When buying a new reel and if undecided on which brand to choose, the golden rule is – if the tackle man knows his stuff, take his advice and if he doesn't, DON'T.

In match fishing you will meet men who swear by one type of reel and who will have nothing to do with any other. Many match anglers from the Leeds, York, Newark and Nottingham areas, for instance, stick fervently to a centre-pin for all of their float fishing, while further south the London-area men nearly always plump for one of the more-modern fixed-spool versions. In all parts of the country, however, there are mixed feelings about reels. In fact in years gone by, there have been challenge matches between the centre-pin-only men and the fixed-spool brigade. More recently – and more pleasing, I think – there have been centre-pin-only contests organised on the middle reaches of the River Trent. If nothing else, these types of event will encourage match newcomers to persevere and be proficient with the 'old wheel'. Personally, I carry all three types of reel on all my match outings, reserving the centre-pin for roach, dace and bleak off the rod end; the open-faced fixed-spool for all my legering and long-distance heavy-float fishing for fish such as bream, barbel and chub; and the closed-faced versions for average float presentation at rivers like the Trent, Severn and Witham. Luckily, I am well off so far as reels are concerned, and I often carry a spare of the type which is likely to be most useful. For a match at a venue like the wide Relief Channel in Norfolk where bream on leger are likely to be a winner, I would carry a spare fixed-spool. On the other hand, I always carry two closed-face reels to the Trent. Have a spare reel close at hand on a really important day, and it could be worth its weight in gold.

The simplest reel of them all is the centre-pin, with no folding handle, slipping clutch or sophisticated gears to go wrong. A centre-pin is basically a revolving drum, usually caged in to a varying extent, and with an audible check. Some of the better ones are also fitted with an adjustable drag, which can be set to suit various flows.

There are two ways of casting out with a centre-pin. My way (being a right-hander) is to cast out and at the precise moment start the drum revolving with the left hand. The other method is to pull loops of line from the

Reels: closed-face, fixed-spool, centre-pin

reel with the left hand, and release them as the rod is swung forward. All this may sound fairly simple, but it isn't at all easy to learn. I was lucky and was weaned on a centre-pin before I was ten years old. Nevertheless, I can understand why some men have tried a centre-pin and given up in desperation.

If you want to see centre-pin experts in action, your best chances are around Nottingham on the River Trent. In fact, walk along the city's Victoria Embankment on any weekend during the season and you will see dozens of locals 'batting' in with an 'old wheel'. Batting, as it is known among Nottinghamshire centre-pin exponents, is a way of reeling line onto the drum without even touching the handles. Southerners may be surprised to find that some Trentsiders don't even have any handles on their centre-pin reels. They take them off so that they don't get in the way while the line is being batted. This method is fairly simple, you just flick and spin the rim of the reel, and the line comes in very fast. A newcomer trying this method for the first time, however, would no doubt have some fun and games if an unexpected monster fish was on the end of his line.

Even among the top-flight match anglers in this country, it is perhaps a little surprising that there are a few who never even consider carrying, let alone using, a centre-pin reel. Perhaps they should cast their minds back to a memorable day in October 1972. Facing extremely stiff opposition in a Woodbine Challenge Final on the roach-filled River Guden in Denmark, fellow Yorkshireman Malcolm Wrigglesworth of Leeds took top prize of £2,000 using – yes – a centre-pin reel. In his net at the finish was a total of 126½ lb, all taken in just 5 hours! Who said centre-pins are out of date?

After fixed-spool reels were first mass-produced, it took quite a few years for them really to catch on, yet today this type is by far the most popular. The greatest advantage is that they allow you to cast long distances with the minimum of effort. In fact, given an hour or so of tuition from an expert, a newcomer could be pushing 30 yards or so of line out, and even landing a float or bomb right onto the far-off grassy bank of a river like the Welland. Not that a novice is likely to catch anything other than sheep or cows from that far-off slope, but it does happen now and again, and is ample proof that the fixed-spool is fairly easy to operate. Later on I shall be dealing with the latest types of closed-faced reels, but first of all, let us take a look at the orthodox open-face ones, the kind you will be using on bream waters where far-off float fishing or swingtip leger tactics will be called for.

Generally, the more money you pay for a reel, the better quality you are likely to get. First and foremost, the reel should be really smooth running when you turn the handle. Remember, if it is a bit rough when you handle it in a tackle shop, the odds are that it could grind to a halt after a season or so of groundbait and sand treatment. Also, try the bale arm action. Make sure it closes over the line every time, before handing over your money. Try the smoothness of the slipping clutch, too. Some reel makers refer to this as drag, but by either name, make sure it can be adjusted to protect the weakest of nylon lines. Unfortunately, too many slipping clutches – even on the more modern reels – need a bit of a jerk to set them slipping. In the world of match fishing, where line breaking strains sometimes go as low as ¾ lb, a sticking clutch can indeed be costly, and I hope the reel manufacturers will resolve this problem.

Whichever brand of fixed-spool you choose, make sure that you can reach the tip of the spool with the forefinger of your rod-holding hand. Unfortunately, most tackle-makers' instructions – and even more unfortunately, some angling writers – tell you to hook the line under your finger before casting out. In that case, of course, it wouldn't matter if the reel spool was a fair distance away from the rod. My way, though, is to flick open the bale arm, put my finger on the lip of the spool, then lift that finger away just at the right moment on the forward cast. It is much easier than messing about hooking your finger under the line. That idea may be necessary in sea fishing where lead weights in excess of 2 and 3 ounces are called for, but I am amazed that it ever caught on at all in our against-the-clock sport. Anyway, try it my way and you will soon find the difference.

When buying a brand new fixed-spool reel, make sure match-type spools are available to fit it. On many so-called match reels, you would require between 500 and 1,000 yards of 2 or 3 lb breaking strain line to bring it to near the lip of the spool. Those types of spool are much too deep, but some manufacturers are now offering shallow spools which are just right, and need only around 100 yards of fine monofilament to fill them to the correct level. Incidentally when the spool is properly filled, the line should be between $\frac{1}{16}$ and $\frac{1}{8}$ inch below the forward lip. It helps, too, I think, if you build the line up a little at the rear side of the spool. In match fishing, the little things count, and I am sure that by having the line on the spool 'sloping down', smoother casting can be achieved. If you have a deep spool and only 100 yards of fine line to put on it, you can of course use wool or string for backing. When joining the nylon line to it, however, ensure that the knot is tucked well out of harm's way.

Many of the better-quality fixed-spool reels have push-button quick-detachable spools – a big help for competition angling. Armed with various spools loaded with different breaking strain lines, you can switch between

Fixed-spool reel and a useful match bream

2, 3 or 4 lb lines in a matter of seconds. Whatever you do, don't have one of the reel's spools loaded with a heavy line of say 12 or 15 lb breaking strain and use it for sea fishing. Freshwater reels are not usually made to withstand the corrosion of salt water. Also, while it is often difficult, try to avoid sand and dirt getting into the gears and bearings. Regularly cleaned and oiled, a quality reel should last at least a few busy match seasons. With some of the popular makes, you can send them back for an overhaul every year or so, and this is a good idea.

A good way of cutting down wear on reel and rod rings is to 'pump' big fish towards the net. Instead of just holding the rod and reeling in, here's how to do it when a decent-size bream is on the line. Slowly raise the rod without reeling, then lower the rod towards the water while reeling in, then raise the rod again and keep repeating this until the fish is close enough to slide into a waiting landing net. Of course, if you used this method to bring a 2-ounce roach to your hand, you would be wasting time. While on the subject of time, don't be obsessed with the idea of high-retrieve gear ratios on fixed-spool reels. Some reels bring in almost 30 inches with one turn of the handle and are perfect for skimming in tiny fish. But never forget, a higher gear ratio will give you less 'feel' when a big fish is tugging away. Going to the extreme, I've no doubt that the manufacturers could design us a match reel with a retrieve twice as fast as any we have now, but it would be useless for swingtipping out bream for instance.

Moving on to the closed-face type, I feel sure that this reel will become increasingly popular, especially on match-type flowing waters where fish like roach and dace are the quarry. Even many former centre-pin exponents have switched over to closed-face fishing, and there is little doubt that it wins money. It may not be the best when roach and bleak are in a feeding frenzy on the surface under the rod end, and I don't use this type for far-off bream on leger, but I am convinced that it is ideal for all other kinds of situations. I use all three types of reel, but if I had to carry just one, it would be a closed-face.

On the one I use – an ABU model – you simply press on the front button and the line is released. There are no bale arm screws for the line to get caught up in or trapped, and only rarely does the line get behind the spool. Trotting down with a closed-face reel is really easy, and despite what some old-timers with an 'old wheel' may say, it is the most efficient way. You press on the button, cast out, put the forefinger back on to the front to trap the line, and slowly move the rod round to follow the float. When the rod has moved round as far as possible, take the finger away from the line, sweep the rod upstream, trap the line again, and so on. All this time, the pick-up in the reel is in the open position. If a fish gives a bite during this trotting down, you simply strike (the finger already has the line trapped) and reel in to engage the pick-up. Done properly, there isn't a fraction of slack line to enable the hook to come free. Remember though, you must keep the finger on the front of the reel when you strike at a bite. What is most pleasing about fishing with my kind of closed-face reel, is that you can cast out and bait the swim – all at the same time.

3 FLOATS

I'm utterly convinced that as far as floats are concerned, it pays to be really organised, have them all graded, and be able to tell at a glance what amount of shot each one will support. I have dozens of floats of all shapes and sizes in my collection, yet as soon as I pick any one of them, I know whether it will carry four 'swans', two AAA, a BB and a number 4, or merely a couple of tiny 'dust' shot. Certainly there are good match anglers who are slap-happy with floats and who don't bother to mark or code them in any way. It is equally certain, however, that these same experts would be even more proficient if they got their float boxes really sorted out. You have to remember that in a match you have only 4, 5 or 6 hours, and every minute you spend sorting through floats at the waterside is another minute less with your bait in the water. In my early years of match fishing there were times when I was just a fish behind the winner, yet I know now that I would have finished a few fish in front if my tackle box and my fishing had been only half as organised as it is today. As one who started in small club matches and then competed against continentals in the World Championships, I can vouch for the fact that odd minutes and odd fish can make all the difference between success and failure.

Float choice. Bill Bartles gives a newcomer some advice

The best thing after making or buying a float is to try it out in a bucket of water. Keep adding or taking off shots until you know exactly what weight it will carry. The most straightforward way, of course, is to write the shot-carrying capacity on the side of each float, and then coat it with clear waterproof varnish. The method I use is to have a colour chart under the lid of the tackle box, with a list of colours on the lefthand side, and a list of shottings on the right. Opposite black, for instance, is BB; white – AAA; and blue – 3BB. Each float is then marked with the appropriate colour. I either use a small band of paint on the stem or glue a coloured plastic float ring onto it. If I want to change to a slightly heavier or lighter float, it is a two-second job to find the right one.

Some matchmen go the whole hog and have complete tackle rigs made up; float, hook and shots. In my ever-full basket, space forbids me going to this extreme, but it is a method used by the top men on the Continent, and judging from their speed successes, it must be worthwhile.

The best way to build a suitable collection of match floats is to make them yourself. Apart from saving yourself quite a bit of money, you can make them any size you wish, and in just the right proportions. It doesn't take long to make a few floats. It would if you tried to get them as smooth, glossy and brightly-coloured as mass-produced ones in the shops, but this glitter – as in the case of shiny rod whippings and chromium-plated reel fittings – is to catch you, and not the fish. In fact the best finish of all on any float is matt. A few of my floats are painted with a bright red or orange tip, but mostly they are black all over, or with just a band of white added near the top. In running water when you are trotting down close-in, an all-black float is a distinct advantage, for as it moves downstream, you can only see the part that is sticking out of the water. As a last resort, in unusual shadings on the water, you can try on various float caps, yellow, white and red, but on most wide-open match waters I rarely find them necessary.

On the subject of float tips, it should be remembered that the more float you have above the water's surface, the less sensitive any tackle rig becomes. Luckily my eyesight is as sharp as a needle and for a lot of my fishing I have the float almost under to start with. Obviously a low-shotted float takes less pulling under than one that is sticking out like a sore thumb. It all depends on the circumstances, and unless you had exceptional eyes, you would need more than just the tip of a float showing if it were cast across to near the far bank on a river like the Nene or the Welland. Also, if the wind is blowing and there are waves on the surface, it will pay to use slightly less shot than usual on any particular float.

Some anglers actually believe that provided a float is well shotted down in the water, the amount of bulk underneath has nothing to do with sensitivity. In a number of match articles in the angling press, it has been stated that a big float shotted down to near the tip is exactly the same as a tiny float shotted down to the same position. Take my tip and ignore such rubbish. If it were so – taking things to an extreme – a submarine submerged with a tiny antenna sticking up out of the water would be as sensitive as a crow's quill. On the basis of my experiences alone, I strongly advise you not to use a big float if a small or medium one will allow you to present a bait just as well. Anyway, let us next take a look at some of the floats I recommend. In doing so, I shall be assuming that where necessary you will be prepared to make them yourself, not just because they will be better than most mass-produced ones, but because some of them may not be available commercially at all.

STICK FLOAT

When these floats first came on to the match scene, they were often regarded as angling gimmicks. Now the majority of top-class contest anglers have a selection of these cane and balsa floats in their tackle boxes. First and foremost, they were perfected by roach anglers, and it is quite a number of years since this type of float first hit the headlines as a winner on the River Trent. But it isn't only on the Trent that this float has made an impact. Years ago, matchmen started winning

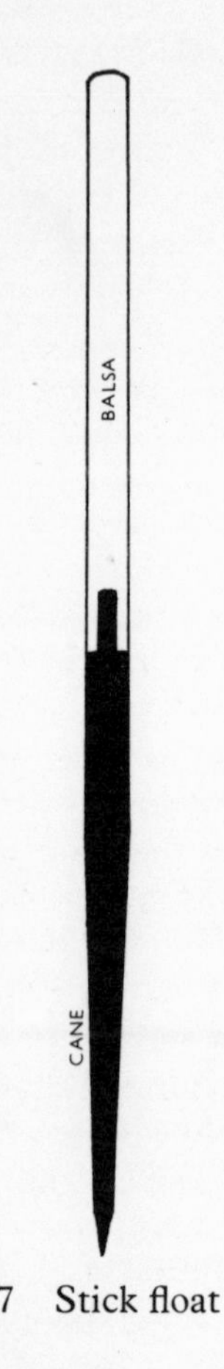

7 Stick float

with this float on the mighty Severn, and the stick float revolution eventually spread south to the Thames.

More recently, the stick float has really proved a money spinner in big matches. Going back to 1972, Phil Coles of Leicester became the youngest-ever angler to win a national championship match with a magnificent display of skill on the Bristol Avon. Using a stick float supporting six AAA shots in only four feet of water, he hammered out 33 lb 8 oz, including chub to around 3 lb, and pocketed close on £2,000.

And just a year later in September 1973, Alan Wright of Sandbach, Cheshire, left the Lincolnshire and South Yorkshire swingtip experts dumbfounded by winning a national championship on the breamy River Witham using a stick float. Fishing with tackle more familiar on the Trent – a 'stick' supporting only a BB and a number 4 shot – he netted 18 bream for a total of 41 lb 10 oz from his swim upstream of Langrick Bridge. He too collected around £2,000 and proved again that the stick float will be with us for a very long time to come. That 41 lb 10 oz net on a stick float, by the way, is the biggest catch ever in a Witham national.

Why is it, you may ask, that the stick float is so effective on rivers such

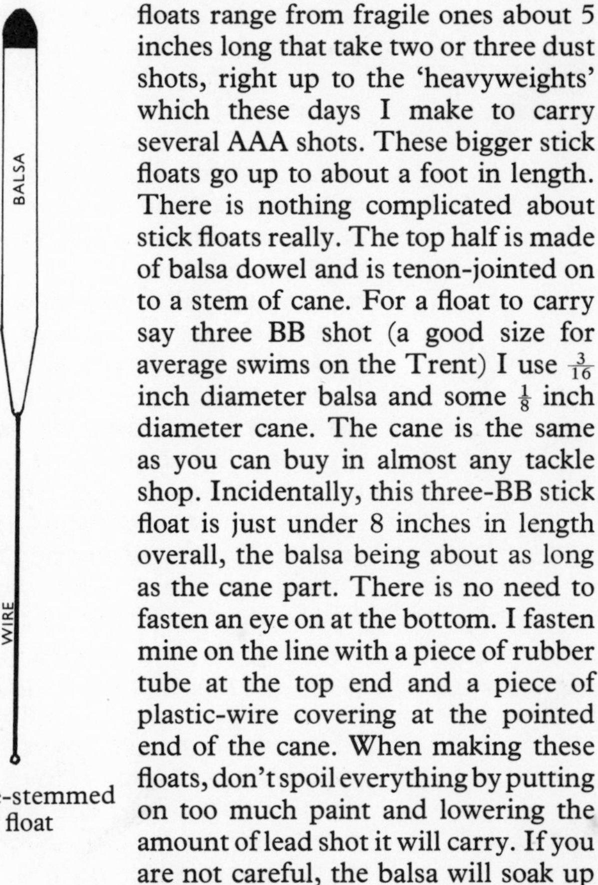

8 Wire-stemmed stick float

as the Trent? Its main asset is that it is thinner at the bottom than at the top and casts out pretty well. My stick floats range from fragile ones about 5 inches long that take two or three dust shots, right up to the 'heavyweights' which these days I make to carry several AAA shots. These bigger stick floats go up to about a foot in length. There is nothing complicated about stick floats really. The top half is made of balsa dowel and is tenon-jointed on to a stem of cane. For a float to carry say three BB shot (a good size for average swims on the Trent) I use $\frac{3}{16}$ inch diameter balsa and some $\frac{1}{8}$ inch diameter cane. The cane is the same as you can buy in almost any tackle shop. Incidentally, this three-BB stick float is just under 8 inches in length overall, the balsa being about as long as the cane part. There is no need to fasten an eye on at the bottom. I fasten mine on the line with a piece of rubber tube at the top end and a piece of plastic-wire covering at the pointed end of the cane. When making these floats, don't spoil everything by putting on too much paint and lowering the amount of lead shot it will carry. If you are not careful, the balsa will soak up paint almost to the core. My way is to coat the float with a quick-drying waterproof glue, let it set hard, then paint over.

Using a formula of half balsa, half cane, you can soon equip yourself with a set of 'sticks' to suit a wide variety of swims. It should be noted, however, that these types of float are almost exclusively for use in flowing water. Certainly, I would never consider putting one of these on the line at a stillwater lake. Ideal conditions for using a stick float are when roach or dace are feeding in midwater and taking a falling bait. Under these circumstances I use half a dozen or so number 6 shots and string them out between hook and float. As an alternative to cane and balsa sticks, I sometimes carry a few with wire stems. Some experts prefer them to the orthodox type of stick float, and I have done particularly well with them on the tidal reaches of the Trent around Dunham. Stick floats of both kinds work perfectly on a river like the Trent when there is a soft wind blowing over your shoulder and slightly upstream, but as you may have already found, match fishing waters are not always in such a friendly mood. Here are my final tips for stick float users; don't use them in stillwater, don't use them for laying-on, and always fasten them on the line 'double-rubber'.

ANTENNA

The basic antenna float I am going to deal with here has a cane stem and a body of balsa at the bottom. In complete contrast to the flowing-water range of stick floats, these are brought into action only when the current is sluggish or non-existent. Initially, they were designed for catching far-off bream on waters like the River Welland, River Nene and Huntspill River. More recently they have been used in smaller sizes for catching roach, and I find them ideal for perch fishing on my local reservoir. My set of antenna floats ranges from ones that carry just one AAA shot to the more bulky specimens that take three swans to trim them down. The larger antennas go up to about a foot in length and have an $\frac{1}{8}$ inch diameter cane stem, while the smallest ones are 6 inches long and have a stem of only $\frac{1}{16}$ inch.

These ordinary antenna floats are not loaded in any way, and are ideal for presenting a bait trailing the bottom or just off it. Usually, the bulk shot is nipped-on well up the line towards the float, but there are times, such as when bleak are troublesome, when it pays to put a fair bit of it a foot or so from the hook. Antenna floats really come into their own, I think, when the water is hardly moving, but the surface is being whipped up by a strong wind. On these days you can use an antenna

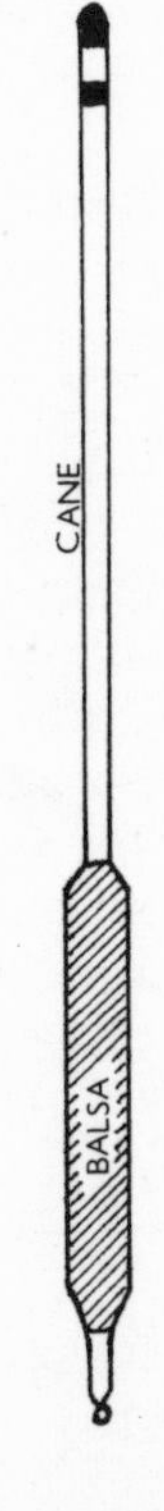

9 Antenna

big enough to allow you to cast out with the minimum of effort, and then the best plan is to sink all of the line between float and rod tip. Sinking the line on rough days is fairly easy, especially when you are using an antenna that carries plenty of shot. Simply cast out to just beyond the baited area, allow the tackle to settle for a few seconds, then dip the rod tip well under the water and give a few sharp turns of the reel.

If you fit these types of float with a tiny wire eye at the bottom – with a hole of only ·015 inches to ·020 inches – they are ideal for using as sliders in deep water. At one time, I had some good bream catches while using this float in conjunction with paternoster tackle. But whenever I am bream fishing these days and the bait has to be anchored far off, I much prefer the more direct way with a leger and no float at all. Lastly on antennas, they should be fastened to the line bottom end only (peg-leg), unless the wind is perfect and coming right over your shoulder.

PEACOCK WAGGLER

Without a doubt, the peacock waggler (or 'swinger' as it is sometimes called) has made a greater impact on the match fishing scene in recent years than any other item of tackle. In point

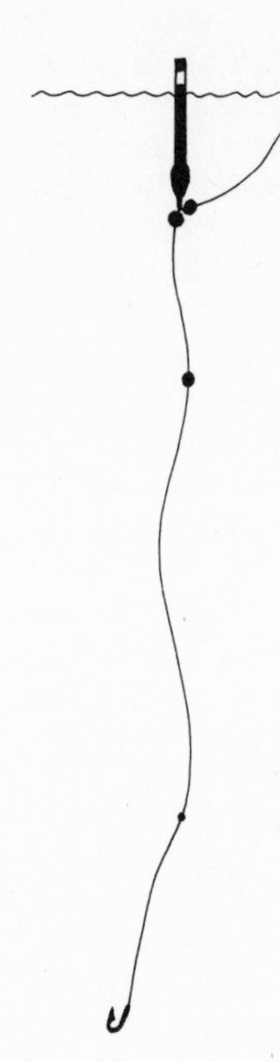

10 Peacock waggler tackle rig

of fact, the peacock waggler is not really new at all. Anglers have been using peacock-stemmed floats for many years. What is different, however, is the variety of ways in which they are used, and whereas years ago they were mostly employed as heavy-shot-carrying antennas on wide bream waters, today's peacocks are also being used with equal success for catching far-off roach on rivers like the Trent and Severn. I still believe that when conditions are good and the fish are feeding off the bottom close-in, in a steady run of water, there is nothing to beat a stick float as far as bait presentation is concerned. On the other hand, clear-water conditions often lead to the fish being well out in midstream, and although you could put on a big stick float and go further out, it often causes complications. For a start, you would get more than your share of line tangles if you pushed a stick float, fastened double-rubber, out 20 or more yards time after time, in an awkward wind. Not only that, the advantage of a stick-float rig is that you can steady the bait as it goes down the swim – only though, if you are fishing reasonably close-in.

The advantage of a waggler then, is that it allows you to cast well out with a minimum of line tangles, and you can sink the line easily to avoid any skimming down-river wind. Certainly you can't hold the tackle back and steady the bait, but by having your bottom shot dragging along the bottom, you get a similar effect. On a good number of match days, of course, you will catch fish after fish on waggler with a bait off the bottom, even though it may be going through the swim pretty fast. On some days, finicky fish will call for a bait being checked by that shot dragging on the river bed, while on others the roach and dace will be bang on feed and it won't matter at all. Naturally, if you are 'dragging along', you will need more float than usual sticking out of the water. Otherwise, it would be submerged much of the time.

My basic rig when waggler fishing is just about as simple as you will ever get. I lock the float with two or three AAA or swan shots (according to the size of the waggler), have an AAA 18 inches to 2 feet below the float, then nip on a number 3 shot (or as much as three BB in a fast deep flow) about 18 inches from the hook. Most important of all, though, the bottom shot must be nearer the hook than the next AAA higher up the line. Neglect this rule, and you will really be in a tangle.

Straight pieces of peacock quill on their own with an eye whipped on to the bottom will be ideal in some match swims, but whenever heavy shotting and really long casting is called for, I use a waggler with a body of balsa built into the bottom. Glue a short length of $\frac{1}{8}$ inch cane into the bottom of a length of peacock quill, glue a balsa body on to the cane, then whip an eye at the end of the cane.

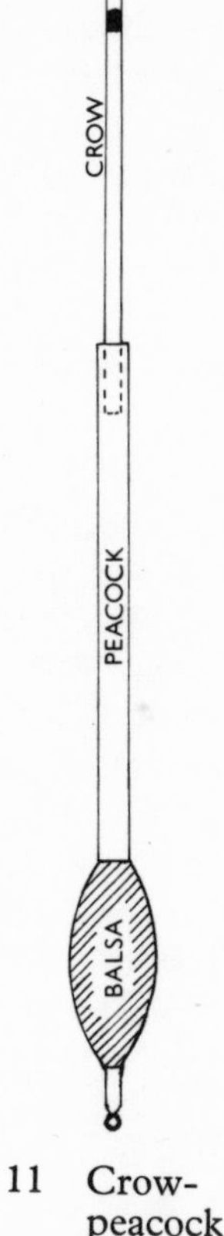

11 Crow-peacock waggler

As an added improvement, I sometimes glue a piece of crow quill into the top of a waggler. Cut off the hollow bottom part of a crow quill, then insert this thick end into the top of the peacock quill. I usually finish up with around $4\frac{1}{2}$ inches of crow quill, giving an overall length of between $7\frac{1}{2}$ and 11 inches. As you will find, this type of waggler is thinner at the top and is more sensitive than the orthodox peacock float. Call it a 'crow-peacock waggler' or whatever you wish, but it certainly is an important part of my float collection.

The trouble is, the demand for peacock quills has led to a severe shortage, but anglers are finding that a replacement material – sarkandas – is equally good if not better. This Indian reed is as light as peacock, a lot straighter, and is much easier to work with. Already sarkandas is being acclaimed as the top float material of this decade – and I'll bet those peacocks strutting about in foreign lands would agree on that!

AVONS

While it is true to say these cane-stemmed floats, with a balsa or cork body well up towards the tip, are less popular than they were 20 or 30 years ago, they remain among the most versatile even in this age of sarkandas and wagglers. You can use them peg-leg fashion for stillwater roach on canals and fenland drains, and I have won quite an amount of money with them fastened double-rubber on the River Trent. In fact, given an awkward wind coming downstream and fish just past the rod end, this float is equal to any and certainly better – under those conditions – than the now-famous stick float.

When making these Avons, there is really no need to fasten a tiny wire eye at the bottom. When using this type peg-leg style, I secure it on the line with a short piece of plastic-wire covering. To use this same float double-rubber, I also push a short section of cycle valve rubber over the tip. You can make them in an unlimited range of sizes, my favourites carrying between one BB and three BB shots.

12 Avon

BALSA

Streamlined floats made entirely of balsa wood allow you to work a bait smoothly just above the bed of a strong-flowing river. I have used them for big nets of winter bream and roach on the River Bure in Norfolk, and many Midland matchmen consider them ideal for the more turbulent stretches of the River Severn. Another river where they allow perfect bait presentation is the Yorkshire Ouse, especially in the deep and fairly narrow sections around Nun Monkton.

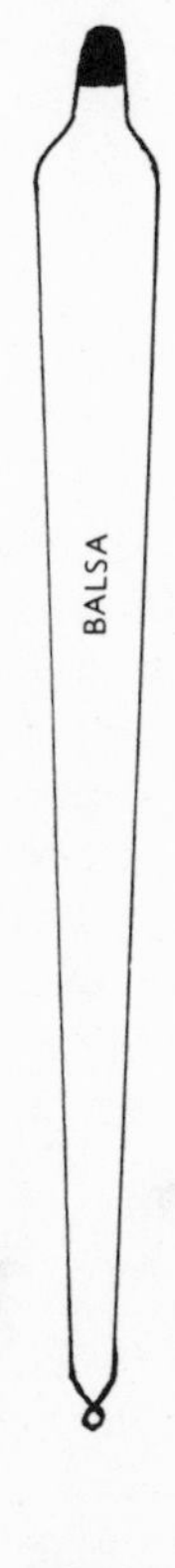

13 Balsa

There is no need to make balsa floats in small sizes supporting just one BB or so, for if I was faced with a swim so smooth as to allow that, I would choose a 'stick' or Avon every time. My range of all-balsa floats starts with a toddler that takes one AAA shot, while the big boys carry four swans.

All my balsa floats are fitted with a wire eye at the bottom, and this makes sure they do not slide down the line. I pass the line through a top float rubber, then through the eye, and then put a BB on the line just at the bottom of the float. This wire eye and shot idea prevents loss of big bulky floats, and makes sure the depth setting is held secure.

Balsa floats – and big Avons as well – can be fitted with two tiny eyes (the same ones I advised for the bottom of the Antenna) to allow them to be used as sliders. In this case, in addition to the usual eye at the extreme bottom of the balsa, you have to put another on the side of the float about ½ inch from the top. Where a swim goes 14 or 15 feet and more, this sliding float idea on running water can give a distinct advantage. Otherwise, though, I much prefer to have a balsa locked on the line – even if it entails using a 13 foot rod or one a bit longer.

ZOOMER

Basically this type of float is an antenna with some loading built into the bottom. Judging from the way they fly through the air to the far side of a river like the Welland, it isn't surprising that they became known as zoomers. While these floats are loaded with lead or brass at the bottom just above the eye, they should never be self-cocking. In fact, I would not make any kind of float into a self-cocker, for it would make it extremely difficult to spot a bite 'on the drop'.

And it is when far-off bream and roach are taking a falling bait that this float really comes into its own. However, the zoomer is a calm-water float and is difficult to hold steady among high waves. In rough conditions, a peacock waggler or ordinary antenna would give you a better chance of winning on a wide match water.

On the right day, though, the zoomer is easy to use, most of the bites being shown by a lift of the float as the bream and roach grab the bait in mid-water. It is essential when using this type of float – for the fishing it was designed for – to have a 'tell-tale' shot no smaller than a number 2, about 18 inches from the hook. The bulk shot – which in this case should be very little – should be positioned not far under the float. You can use these floats fastened on the line bottom only, but they are far more effective, and really dart out, if fished double-rubber.

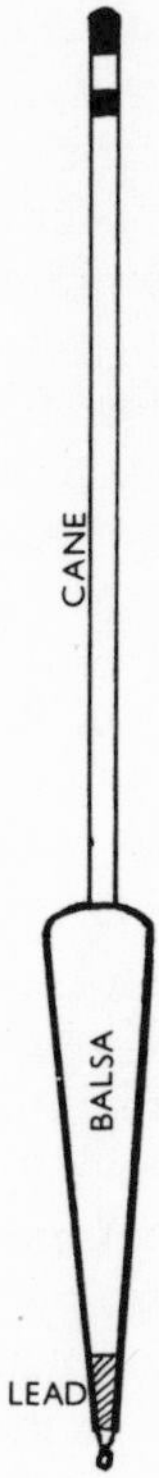

14 Zoomer

PIMPER

This type of float is by far the smallest in my range of floats, yet it is one of the most useful, especially when there are hordes of tiny bleak, dace or roach near the surface, and other species like bream and chub show no sign of coming round for dinner. To be quite honest, there is nothing I like better than to win with a tiny float under the rod tip while all the others are bashing away with big floats or heavy Arlesey bombs. It is the total weight of fish that counts – not the species – and that is why the bleak-catching pimper float is so often a winner.

Only 4 or 5 inches in length, these pimpers have a slender cane stem with a tiny body of cork or balsa. Certainly you won't be able to cast great distances as you would with a zoomer or waggler, but if you don't have the tiny fish feeding close-in, the odds are you won't catch enough of them anyway. Fastened on the line mostly double-rubber, these tiny floats support hardly any weight at all. My smallest carries one number 6 shot, and the largest needs only a number 1 to trim it down. Win with this float and you will probably be dubbed a 'pimper', but you will not bother about that as they hand you the cup and the money. In fact, you will laugh all the way to the bank!

CORK

CANE

15 Pimper

GRAYLING STICK

16 Grayling stick

Every so often in match fishing, we find ourselves confronted with a boily sort of swim, such as the edge of a bay when the river is in flood. Normal tactics on these days are often hopeless, and you have to have a float that will stand up to the strong undercurrents, yet at the same time be fairly streamlined. As the name implies, this float was invented by me with grayling in mind. Nevertheless, it has often proved worthwhile in turbulent roach swims and it is always likely to be a 'saver' on those flood-water match outings when everything seems hopeless.

Grayling sticks, mind you, have little in common with grayling 'bobs', the most horrible float ever designed. Compared with a 'bob' which has a bulbous body, my version is as streamlined as any float of this size can be. The construction of it is fairly straightforward, as it is simply a stick float of cane and balsa, with a tapered body of cork glued on. My favourite grayling stick supports two swan shots, and is 7 inches in length.

CROW QUILL

Going back 30 years and more, almost every angler in Sheffield fished with crow quills, and yet today many of the tackle shops in that steel city do not find it worthwhile to stock them. While we do not hear of many match wins on crow quills these days, it is undoubtedly one of the most pleasant floats to use. For me, crow-quill fishing brings back happy memories. In my teenage years I won nine club matches in ten weeks, all on the same float, and it is still in my tackle box.

The most useful sizes are those that carry between one BB and one AAA. The biggest drawback with these floats is that they are not easy to cast out. Nevertheless, some top anglers around Newark in Nottinghamshire are convinced that this float is still best on the Trent. They could be right, too, and who knows – after a few big wins on this float in the next year or two – there may even be complaints of a crow quill shortage, or even a crow shortage!

PORCUPINE

Again, we come to a running-water float, the 'porky' as it is often referred to along the river banks. It is a float that is favoured by match experts in the Nottingham areas, and, as you would expect, they mostly use it on the nearby River Trent. It is a buoyant streamlined float and is a type – in various sizes – that can be employed at rivers as varied and as far apart as the Tees and the Thames. The porcupine is much tougher and far less likely to be broken than most other types of quill, and this is perhaps one of the reasons why it has remained popular.

Personally, I have always reserved these floats for waters with some flow, fastening them on the line double-rubber. Some match expert colleagues of mine cut off the pointed tips of 'porkys', making them very much like a stick float in appearance. I have recently tried this 'blunt-end' idea, and I am sure it is an improvement for waters that have a strong pull.

The biggest complaint against porcupine floats is that they are awkward to cast out and cause many line and hook length tangles. True, these floats tend to be a bit top-heavy, though I get over most of this problem by nipping some lead shot on the line right at the bottom of the stem. They still don't go out like a dart, but at least it is an improvement.

Buying a set of porcupine floats is never an easy business. They vary so much and you can get one 9 inches long that will support one swan shot, and yet you may find another of the same length that will carry almost twice as much weight.

WIGAN SPECIAL

Over in Lancashire, this special float was perfected solely for the job of presenting a bloodworm on delicate tackle on the far-off fringes of those really difficult canals in that area. Many years ago the light-tackle experts of the Wigan district found that their tiny perch – and even the gudgeon – were often reluctant to take baits hung on thick nylon or suspended beneath heavy floats. And so the Wigan special was born, a float for really special anglers who, on their hard canals, have to be extra skilful to make up for the shortage of fish.

The first time I came across the Wigan special float was, as you may guess, at Wigan – Higher Ince to be exact. It was there that I was introduced to John Hilton, and it was he who demonstrated the use of the Wigan float on a local water. Actually, I was preparing to fish in a World Championship match on the Danube in Hungary, and was getting in some close-season practice with John, and at the same time obtaining the benefit of his experience with bloodworms.

Briefly, the Wigan float is probably the forefather of the Trent stick float. The only difference is that the stem is much more slender and instead of an equal length of balsa and cane, the canal version only has a small length of balsa – about an inch or so – on top

17 Wigan special

of the cane. The weight of the cane almost cancels out the buoyancy of the balsa, and rarely are more than two dust shots needed on the hook length. For this type of float to be really effective, of course, it has to be trimmed right down in the water – 'dotted' – as they say west of the Pennines.

CROW ZOOMER

Of my own float designs, creations, inventions or discoveries – call them what you will – the one I am most pleased with is the crow zoomer. When I first made this float a few years ago, I wasn't thinking in terms of specific gravities of materials or anything like that, but now I know that I hit on a winner. It is made of two of my favourite float-making materials, balsa and bird quill. It has helped me to fill a net on countless occasions, and although all other floats go under at some time, this crow zoomer of mine gives the impression that once it starts going down it will carry on until it hits the river bed!

Certainly this float is not lacking in versatility. I have used it for perching days on my local reservoir, loose-floated it peg-leg style for Middle Level bream, and used it double-rubber just over the weed fringe at the River Witham to take match nets of roach on hempseed and tares. I make this type of float in a number of sizes, the best being those that carry somewhere between one AAA and one swan shot.

Although I have larger crow zoomers taking up to nearly two swans, none of them are bulky in any way, in fact they are among the most streamlined of all floats. The main body or lower part of this float is made of balsa, the top of it reduced to about $\frac{1}{8}$ inch diameter, onto which is glued the hollow top half of a big crow quill. A tiny wire eye is whipped on at the bottom end of the float, and then I load it slightly at the bottom of the balsa with a few turns of fuse wire. Give it a light coat of waterproof paint, and you have a float that will – on average – beat all others.

18 Crow zoomer

4 SHOTS AND LEGER WEIGHTS

Although we only buy a packet or so of split shot and a few Arlesey bombs and other leger weights in a season, they all mount up to a fair total as far as tackle businesses are concerned. In fact one firm alone melts down about 2 tons of lead every year to produce a variety of fishing weights. Assuming that anglers lose a large proportion of this total while actually fishing, there must be a great deal lying on our river beds. While there are many fishing weights produced by different firms, it is a pity that such a large proportion – particularly the split shot – is of poor quality.

In match angling especially, you want to be sure that shot will stay put in one place, and at the same time you want to be able to remove it from the line fairly easily. All too often, I'm sorry to say, the lead is either too hard or cut too deep. Take my tip, test split shot before you buy it and make sure it is only cut slightly more than halfway through. Some shot is bright and shiny when you buy it, although it soon becomes dulled if you carry it around as I do, all mixed up in one box. I have tried the shot-dispenser idea, but I find it a bit too fiddly, especially in freezing conditions in winter.

The largest size shot is swan, or, as it is sometimes called in the trade – SSG. Lower down the weight range, we come to AAA, BB, then numbers 1 right down to number 8, which is dust shot. The bigger the number, the smaller the shot. As a general guide, one swan shot is roughly the same weight as two AAA shot; and one AAA is about the same as two BB. Swan shots should average approximately 15 to the ounce (and are just over ¼ inch in diameter) while at the lower end of the scale, number 8 shot averages about 400 to an ounce. Nowadays, shot number 10 is being imported from the Continent, but this is unlikely to be of any interest unless you are an out-and-out bleak snatcher. Also available are 'mouse droppings', small oval-shaped leads which can be useful when hemp fishing. In theory, when fish are biting madly on hempseed, they are likely to take an ordinary round shot by mistake. Another alternative is to make your own hemp-fishing shot out of thin sheet lead. Whatever lead you use, never nip it tightly enough to weaken the nylon line.

As there is more legering done in matches these days than ever before, the demand for Arlesey bombs has increased enormously. At one time it was mostly specimen-hunting types who hurled lumps of lead to far-off swims and waited for big fish. But more and more competition men have realised that a legered bait well across can often be a winner for fish like bream. The most useful sizes in Arlesey bombs are ¼ ounce, ⅜ ounce, ½ ounce and ¾ ounce. These popular sizes are usually available in tackle shops, but these days the trend is for anglers to make their own. A number of firms can supply aluminium moulds for this price-cutting operation, but as yet I have not found one that can supply a mould for ¼ ounce Arlesey bombs (or swivel bombs, as they are sometimes called). To get round this problem, some anglers buy a mould for making ¼ ounce Wye leads, and use these on a paternoster link. It is just as easy, I think, to use a couple

Trent chub. These fish were caught on leger tackle with a string of swan shots on a sliding nylon link. The bait was cheese

of swan shot if a $\frac{1}{4}$ ounce bomb is not at hand.

I often use coffin leads when legering far-off in a fast flow, but instead of simply threading them onto the line, I use them on a paternoster-style link of nylon. To facilitate this, I put a split pin through the hole, then bend the ends over. To finish the job properly, it pays to solder over the sharp ends. Ordinary bombs are usually

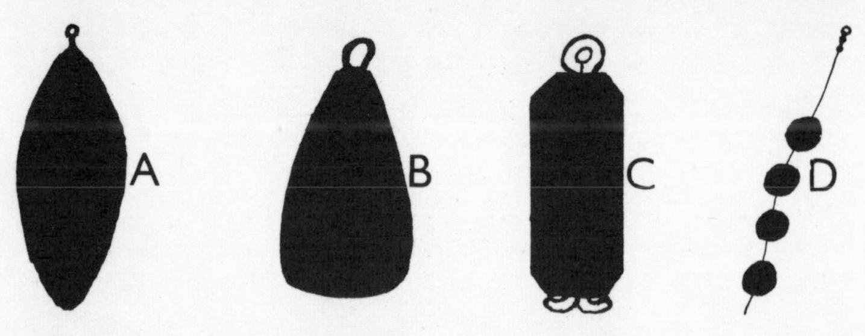

19 Leger weights. (a) Arlesey bomb (b) pear (c) coffin (d) string of swan shots

employed on a fixed or sliding link when we are quiver-tipping or swingtipping, so on most occasions it doesn't really matter whether the piece of pear-shaped or oval lead has a swivel fitted or not.

Hillman-type clip-on leads have never really caught on in match fishing, and there are only a minority of anglers who use 'drilled bullets' these days for legering. On the other hand, there is much to be said for 'Capta' leads, especially at waters where the flow is deep and powerful. These Captas are a sort of pyramid shape with a swivel moulded into one side. These leads stay put much better than any others I have tried, although of course it isn't on every match trip that we want a completely anchored bait. A bait rolling round is often a winner, and for this style I prefer an Arlesey bomb, pear lead, or simply a string of swan shots.

5 HOOKS

When a man decides to take up match fishing seriously, he must face the fact that while many fish such as bream, roach, chub and even tiny ones like bleak are going to stay on the line and win money, a fair number are going to come off the hook and cause disappointment. Lost fish are all part of the game. In fact if all hooked fish stayed hooked and ended in a net, fishing generally wouldn't be half as exciting.

In contest fishing especially, the difference between a lost and a landed fish can be vital. Many times late in a match I have hooked a 2 or 3-pounder and known that this fish meant the difference between success and failure. Mostly, these money-spinners stay on the hook and are eventually put on the scales, but as the fish is being reeled in, I am forever wondering if the hook will hold. If a fish is lost in snag-free open water, it is a fair bet that the hook has come free. Now and then the line may be broken, but this should not happen very often.

With the hook-hold being so important, it is excusable for newcomers to assume that large hooks will lead to more fish and prize money. On the other hand, the first essential is for the fish to take the bait. Generally speaking – especially with baits such as maggot, hempseed and caster – the bigger the hook, the less bites you will get. When you are waiting for a bite, the ideal hook size may be a 22 or 20, yet when the fish takes the bait, you could do with a number 8 or 10 to make sure that it does not come off. It is no use employing a tiny hook simply because it will bring more bites, and it is equally foolish to sit it out with a big hook when the fish are shy and only half-inclined to feed. The main thing in match fishing is the total weight of fish you put on the scales, and you have to choose a hook size that will increase this – not the number of bites or percentage of landed fish.

Of course, most major contests take place on heavily-fished waters, and so on average it pays to err on the side of small hooks. On a hammered match stretch of the Trent or Witham, for instance, you would require smaller hooks than a freelance roach man would use on a pleasure trip to say a Scottish river like the Tweed or Forth.

Very often hook size is a matter of compromise, and often a case of trial and error. The mood of the fish in a match water can change overnight, and while you may have had good sport with a size 16 hook one day, you might have to scale down to a size 20 on the next session. Even during a match, things can alter, and it often pays to change around with hook sizes to suit the feeding moods of the fish. At all times, though, the hook size must be in proportion to the size of the bait. And while sizes 20 and 18 will usually be best for single maggot, a number 10 is often better when luncheon meat is being offered on a chub and barbel venue.

It also pays to take into consideration the species you are seeking. On a particular match river you may find that you have to scale down to a size 20 to catch the roach on single maggot, while at the same time chub are accepting a maggot on a number 16. As you will see, there is no such thing as a perfect hook size for all match outings.

It will depend mainly on how heavily fished the water is; which species are likely to fill the winner's net; the mood of the fish on that particular day; and the bait you are using. Generally, the line thicknesses should be related to the size of the hook, but here again the species have to be considered. It is well-known for instance that chub are careless about line thickness, and roach are just the opposite. Even tiny bleak will sometimes ignore bait attached to a large hook and thick nylon, and it may be necessary to go as small as a number 22 on only a ¾ lb breaking strain line for this species.

When match fishing for fish such as chub and barbel, the type of swim should influence your choice of hook size and the line attached to it. On a clear open stretch there may be room to play one of these big fish to a standstill on fairly small hooks and fine lines, yet if you drew a really snaggy swim you would have to employ tackle which enabled you to bully them out to a certain extent. By the way, while I use spade-end hooks for all the sizes between 22 and 14, I always plump for eyed ones in the larger sizes. Remember, of course, that the bigger the size number, the smaller the hook.

You can buy hooks already tied (or 'dubbed') to nylon, although I strongly advise against this. They are often of poor quality, rather expensive, and are frequently tied to the wrong thickness of nylon line. There are a number of hook-tying aids on the market now, and some are a great help, especially for anglers with clumsy fingers. Personally, I use a small vice which was put on the market by the Milbro firm many years ago, but you rarely see them in the shops these days. To start off, all you need is a hook-tying device, some nylon line, 100 or so hooks, and some paper packets. The main advantage is that you can tie any hook size to whatever breaking strain line you wish. Whichever device you use – or even if you simply

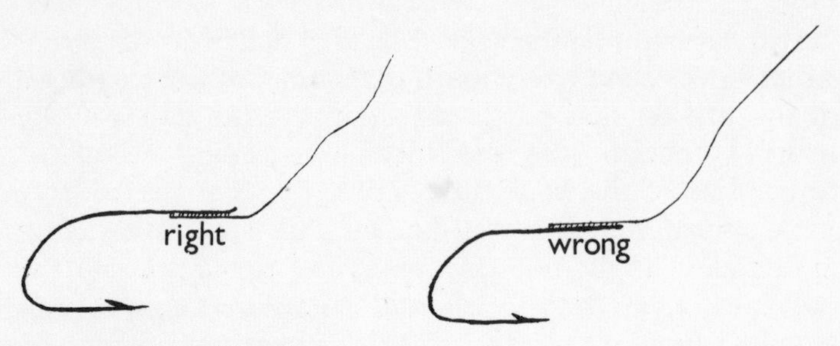

20 Spade end hook

tie them with your fingers – make sure that the line is coming from the inside of the spade end. I tie my spade end hooks to a yard of nylon, and I mark each packet with the size and breaking strain – 22 *x* ¾ lb, 20 *x* 1 lb, 16 *x* 2 lb etc. Eyed hooks, sizes 12 and larger, are fastened on the reel line with a hitched half-blood knot. The gilt straight-eyed hooks I use go under the trade name 'Stiletto'.

There are scores of different type spade end hooks from which to choose, but those I use most these days are Mustad brand pattern number 31380, or V.M.C. (Viellard-Migeon-Cie) number 8408D. If I am in a truly snaggy swim and only catching tiny fish such as gudgeon, I sometimes use a fine wire soft hook (Mustad number 90210). With these I can pull the hook out of a snag, bend the hook over again, and continue fishing. But I would remind you that it is strictly for small fish, and I would never attempt it if some big roach or chub were around.

To quicken things up further, you can use a hook without any barbs. I haven't used them enough to form any firm convictions, but it is likely to speed up unhooking and be worthwhile when hundreds of tiny bleak have to be handled in a few hours. Sheffield specimen hunter Tag Barnes has already caught on to the no-barb idea, so there must be something in it for us matchmen. Tag has taken chub over 3 lb and roach nearing 2 lb on barbless hooks, and some other big-fish men claim to have landed huge carp on them. It certainly makes you think.

Barbs or no barbs, it certainly makes sense to use only sharp hooks. I sharpen my bigger-eyed hooks on a small carborundum stone, but if I suspect that a 22, 20, 18, 16 or 14 hook is at all blunted, I simply scrap it, and put on a new one. By the way – even when there is a large amount of money at stake – never throw a hook away onto the grass, especially if there is a worm or maggot on the end. I have seen a blackbird, starling, thrush and even a robin hung on a tree or tangled in the undergrowth, and I for one – win or lose – have vowed to be particularly careful in future. It doesn't take long to remove the bait off the hook and cut the nylon into small pieces.

I am sorry for digressing a little, but going back to those spade end hooks, here are the hook sizes I use and the permutations of breaking strains I tie them to: size 22 *x* ¾ and 1 lb; size 20 *x* 1 and 1½ lb; size 18 *x* 1, 1½ and 2 lb; size 16 *x* 1½, 2 and 2½ lb; size 14 *x* 2 and 2½ lb. I don't use hooks in sizes smaller than 22. And as outlined earlier, all the eyed hooks – sizes 12 and larger – are tied direct on to the reel line. By the way, always have a good selection of spade end hooks tied up ready for use. It is much better than having to tie spade end knots during a vital contest, especially if the weather is freezing and fingers are numb.

Finally in this chapter, a word about double-hook rigs, and a reminder that in most parts of the country, only one hook can actually be in use at any one time. You can, of course, have a hook on each of the rods ready for use, but that is a different thing altogether. The answer – if you fancy 'double-hooking' – is to check the match rules BEFORE the contest, not after.

The greatest advantage with using, say, two hooks, is

that you could have a maggot on one hook and worm on the other. It could perhaps save time spent swapping and changing with various hooks and baits. In theory it is supposed to give you a distinct advantage over your opponents, but at the waterside I have never yet proved that a two-hook rig produces more weight of fish than just one hook. Don't forget, too, if you have a big fish on the line and another hook dangling free, things can be decidedly dodgy – especially if that big fish happens to be a barbel and there are some tree roots or other snags around!

6 LINES

Almost as regularly as match seasons come and go, new fishing lines appear on the market, and there are all kinds of claims that will have you believe that there has never been anything like it before. In fact if you had gone out and bought every new line that has been advertised in the past decade or so, you would be able to stand on Westminster Bridge and cast right into the middle of the Norfolk Broads – if the reel and leger were big enough!

There really are many lines from which to choose. Some are brown, some green, there are bright blue ones and others with no colour at all. You can go out and buy 200 or 300 yards of one brand, or choose another make of line and get about 2 miles. They start at ¾ lb breaking strain, and line thickness goes far stronger than we matchmen will ever need. In fact, rarely will a line in excess of 5 lb breaking strain ever be required by the average competition man. As explained in the previous chapter, I use nylon line ranging up to 2½ lb as hook lengths. In addition, though, I have a centre-pin reel loaded with 2 lb line, a closed-face reel with 2 lb and 3 lb (two different spools), and an orthodox fixed-spool reel with 3 lb and 4½ lb (again on separate spools).

With normal use, without it being overstretched, I don't think there is usually much deterioration in a nylon line. What I am sure of, however, is that some lines are better than others when you buy them, and it is nothing to do with particular makes, colours, or even the relative prices of the lines. As a matter of fact, the most expensive may not be the best, and the cheapest is unlikely to be the worst.

Mind you, if you have bought a new line and find that it keeps breaking, don't immediately blame the line and send it back to the distributors. It could be a faulty line, admittedly, but first of all, check rod rings and reel bale arm for sharp edges. Not least, of course, make sure that the slipping clutch is set correctly.

After buying a new line, the best thing to do is check its actual breaking strain. Whether you buy your line by the 50 yards, 100 yards or even the mile, at least one thing is almost certain – it will rarely be the same breaking strain as printed on the spool. In recent years I have bought line marked 1½ lb breaking strain that was barely 1 lb; 1 lb that was 1½ lb; a 2 lb that pulled 3 lb; a 2 lb that was actually 1½ lb; and another marked 3 lb that went to 4½ lb.

To a match fishing beginner, ½ lb breaking strain error either way may seem of little consequence, but it is not so. Just imagine what can happen, for example, if you use a reel line marked 2 lb which pulls less than 1½ lb, and a hook length rated 1½ lb which takes a pull of 2 lb. Little wonder we see so many hooks and floats anchored in the middle of a pond or river. After taking off a line which was previously marked 1½ lb and putting on one marked 2 lb, how many anglers realise that they may be reducing the actual breaking strain of their tackle?

It is best then to find out the real strength of the line. A general guide is to measure the line carefully with a micrometer. A nylon line of ·004 inch is roughly 1 lb breaking strain; ·005 inch is about 1½ lb breaking strain, and so on, with 8 lb monofilament measuring about ·012 inch in diameter.

Not everybody has a micrometer handy, and in any case, I have a way which is absolutely infallible. (No, I don't tie on so many ½ lb packets of margarine and try lifting them – for a start, it will always break at the knot!) To test the true breaking strain of line, you want no knots at all, and this is how I do it using a spring balance. Coil the line around the hook of the spring balance at least six or seven times, put the two loose ends together, then pull carefully and gradually increase the tension. It is best to have somebody pulling on the nylon and someone else watching the scales. The line will finally break, and then the mark on the scales will have to be noted. To make absolutely sure, it pays to do this test three times, though you will find that the line from one spool will always break at the same strain. Having concluded that the scales read 2 lb, 3 lb, 5 lb or even as high as 10 lb or so, all you do then is divide this figure by half and you have the true breaking strain of your line without knots or kinks.

Provided you have carried out this line test, and your hook length of nylon is weaker than your reel line, you should never lose a favourite float in the middle of the river. Remember, though, to watch out for knots along the line. Each knot – and there should be as few as possible in any tackle rig – is a weak point. Incidentally, never look at a line and try and guess which is the thickest or strongest. A light-coloured line, for instance, will look much thicker than an identical line in a dark colour such as brown.

After purchasing a new fishing line, many matchmen complain of the line coming off the reel in kinks. Sometimes the manufacturers are at fault, but mostly it is the anglers themselves who have put the kinks in, right at the start when they have transferred the line from the spool on to the reel. There is a wrong way and there is a right way to fill a reel with line. Here is the right way. Get someone to hold the new spool of line by pushing a pencil through the hole in the middle. Fasten the line onto the backing, or the spool, on the reel, and then slowly reel in. If done correctly, the line should pull from the spool as it is turning on the pencil. It pays to put the line on the reel under slight tension.

Whatever you do, don't just throw the spool of line onto the ground and reel in. Another tip – always make sure the knot fastening line to backing or spool is tucked well out of harm's way before reeling on the rest of the line.

7 · NETS

Keepnets over the years have gradually become larger and larger, not just because – as national championship results show – winning catches are getting bigger, and not because present day match anglers are more optimistic than their grandfathers. It is simply that if you take part in a match these days under National Federation of Anglers rules, you must put all your fish in a keepnet of not less than 8 feet in length with a diameter of not less than 15 inches, if it is circular, or not less than 15 inches by 10 inches if it has rectangular rings. That is the ruling on keepnets.

Mind you, it makes sense to carry a large net. On a high awkward bank, for instance, you can have the bottom few rings of the net in the water, yet the neck of the net is still close at hand. When the top of the net is just in front of your knees, vital seconds are not lost in reaching down the bank. On top of that, nothing is more annoying than dropping a fish in the water, and then losing by just half an ounce or so.

Certainly there are many top-class match anglers who consider that even a net of 8 feet in length is not sufficient for some of those really high banks we often find on rivers like the Severn. To cater for these matchmen, a number of tackle companies are now making nets in lengths of 10 feet and 12 feet. Most matchmen – myself included – plump for a net of around 18 inches in diameter. There are keepnets with much bigger diameters, but these are mostly for specimen hunters, and in any case a net bigger than 12 feet by 18 inches would be rather cumbersome to carry along a match length, especially when you are already well loaded with other things such as rods, squats and groundbait. In the old days, most keepnets were fitted with metal rings, but I much prefer the more modern idea of using rings of polythene. All modern nets, by the way, are made of nylon mesh.

On the subject of mesh, a matchman should avoid any keepnet other than one in minnow mesh. This size, if you are in doubt, is about $\frac{5}{16}$ inch between knots and just about large enough to allow a pencil to squeeze through the holes. If you use a so-called 'bream' or 'gudgeon' mesh, you could have a few vital ounces escape through the holes.

Most pleasing, I think, is the shape of the top ring on some modern keepnets. Mine, for instance, has a large circular neck, but it is fitted with a short length of polythene that permits it also to be used as a rod rest. All bank sticks and keepnets are interchangeable, the thread being $\frac{3}{8}$ inch B.S.F. The very latest in keepnets is a nylon type that is absolutely knotless. The makers claim that it causes less damage to fish, and if this is true, it is bound to catch on more among all coarse anglers.

Going on to landing nets now, I don't think there is any need at all for a really large one. In fact, a heavy net would slow things down considerably and be a disadvantage. More care should perhaps be used when choosing a landing net handle. Many so-called telescopic handles can so easily become jammed solid by a few grains of sand, and I much prefer the two-aluminium-pole idea.

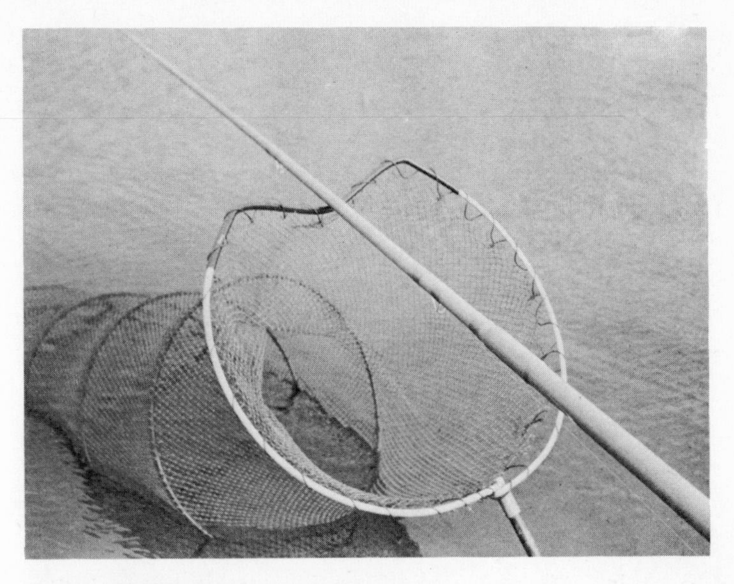

Keepnet being used as a rod rest

You simply screw them together.

A landing net is generally used when the line is not strong enough to lift a big fish out of the water. But in match fishing you cannot afford to take chances, and even with a $\frac{1}{2}$ lb fish on 1 lb line, there is always a chance of the hook tearing out and coming free. Many anglers often do not bother to reach for the landing net because of the messy job of getting a fairly small fish out of the bottom of the deep mesh. The best way – unless you are likely to encounter a real whopper on that particular day – is to twist the bottom of the net and tie a knot in it.

To save time and trouble, simply ladle the fish out of the water with the shallow net, lay the net on the bank, and then lift up the rod and swing the fish into your hands. This way – if the weight of the fish is less than the breaking strain of the tackle – you won't have to fumble in the net to get the fish out. What's more, if the fish does happen to come off the hook between the net and your hands, at least it won't drop back into the water.

Lastly on nets, a warning about mice. If there are any mice within 10 miles of your home, be very careful. For some unknown reason, mice cannot resist nibbling away at nylon nets, and in next to no time they can cause a great deal of damage. A few years ago, I had an almost new keepnet ruined by mice, so I now keep all nets hung up out of their way. And just to make doubly sure, I've now got a large ginger tomcat for a pet.

8 SEAT BASKETS

Most anglers I know have started with a fairly small basket, then have gone on to one of medium size, and finally, especially in the match fishing fraternity, have finished up with a really jumbo-sized one. The best way, I reckon, is to get a large basket right from the beginning. If you have a big one, you don't have to fill it on every trip (although this seems to be the tendency), but the extra space can come in very handy if you are, for example, selected for a national team, or – as I was – asked to represent your country on the Continent. Mind you, a large basket full of bait and tackle can be quite heavy, and it always pays to fit it out with a wide shoulder strap, preferably well padded.

Wickerwork baskets in the tackle shops usually start at a size of 17 inches in length, 11 inches wide, and about 12 inches high; absolutely useless I would think, except for a young angler who was not very big himself. The largest in the range is often 22 inches long, 14 inches wide and 15 inches high. Luckily, I managed to get one made to my own specifications, and if you can persuade someone to do the same for you, here are the dimensions: 22 inches long, 16 inches wide and 16 inches high. All the basket sizes I have given, by the way, are outside measurements. Incidentally, if your choice is a large basket, always buy one of those with six legs as they are far more stable.

Apart from allowing you to fit in a special float box and bait-mixing bowls, a jumbo-sized basket is often the most comfortable of all on which to sit. With a high basket, in particular, your legs are not cramped up. As an added aid to comfort, I always carry a large piece of 2 inch thick foam rubber. The only snag likely with a monster-sized basket, is if it is too big to fit into the boot of your car. There is only one cure for that – choose a van or car to suit the size of your basket and rod holdall. That is what I do, anyway.

A big problem these days is finding large baskets which are really well made from English willow or strong cane. Many of today's fishing baskets are imported and do not come up to the standard of 'made in Britain' ones.

When the bottom of my old basket was breaking up, I was faced with high replacement costs, and it was then I discovered that baskets in many shops were certainly not what they used to be. I put off the job of finding a good new one after a few visits to tackle shops, but the inevitable happened – the bottom fell right out. Six years of regular use had seen it wedged on the rocky banks of the Trent, leant over on sloping banks like those at the Middle Level Drain, and half submerged to act as a bait table on the River Severn. From my local Dam Flask Reservoir to the far-off Danube, it had taken a lot of hammering and it was a real wonder that it lasted out as long as it did.

Realising that I was unlikely to find a suitable replacement because the old one had been made to order to my own requirements, I decided that some kind of repair was necessary. I didn't fancy parting with my old faithful that I'd sat on for hundreds and hundreds of hours, and to be honest, I didn't fancy the idea of forking out a lot of money for a new one. After all, you can get a very great amount of maggots for the price of a new basket!

Anyway, if you have a basket with the bottom hanging out or held together with pieces of string, here is how to make a professional-type repair at very low cost. What is more, the old basket will be as firm and as strong as it was when you first got it, maybe more so.

First of all, buy a piece of good-quality $\frac{1}{4}$ inch plywood, a fraction bigger than the outside measurements of the bottom of the basket. The only other expense will be of four or six rubber door stops, and the same number of wood screws (2 inches x $\frac{3}{16}$ inches). If your basket – like mine – has six legs, you will need six rubber stops and screws, but if the basket has only four legs, then four of each will suffice.

The next step is to take the bottom of the basket out altogether. Perhaps it has fallen off already, but if not, cut the remaining pieces of intact willow or cane. Then stand the basket on something really flat. The dining room table will be ideal, but first – better make sure your wife is out of the way! After standing for hours on flat outhouse floors at home, most baskets are fairly level, but if one leg is shorter than the others, mark it. After that, you have to saw off the protruding parts of the legs, just about level with the bottom of the wickerwork. On my basket I had to cut $1\frac{1}{2}$ inches from each leg. Before making any cuts, though, take into account any unevenness in the legs. If, for instance, one leg was $\frac{1}{4}$ inch shorter than the others, you would cut $\frac{1}{4}$ inch less off that particular one, and vice versa.

With the legs sawn off level with the bottom, stand the basket on the plywood, position it in the correct place, and mark around the legs with a pencil. Take away the basket, and you will have a piece of plywood with four or six circles marked on it. In the centre of each circle on the plywood, drill a $\frac{3}{16}$ inch hole, then put the plywood back onto the basket in the same position as before. Hold it there firmly, then mark the bottom of the legs with the drill going through the plywood. After that, drill a $\frac{1}{16}$ inch hole into each leg to give a start to the screws. It is then a simple job to complete the repair. Just place the plywood into position, put one of the rubber door stops over each hole, and secure a screw into each one.

From start to finish, the job only took me half an hour. I was so pleased, I even gave the plywood three coats of polyurethane paint to keep out the wet. Besides being slightly more roomy than ever, it is now a smart-looking tackle carrier. Not bad, really, when you consider that all it cost was the price of six screws, six doorstops and a piece of plywood.

Having made it clear that I much prefer a large wicker-

Fishing basket before repair

work basket for carrying tackle to a match peg, I realise, nevertheless, that some of the combination seat-haversacks are actually preferred by a few matchmen. For a disabled angler, for instance, a seat carrier with a backrest can make match fishing possible when otherwise it might not be. Perhaps those carriers with a steel frame and waterproof material would be more popular if they were mostly the right shape to take things like tackle boxes and bait mixing-bowls. And a complaint against some seat-haversacks with backrests is that they sink too easily into bankside mud.

Leaving aside these criticisms of combination seats, match angling is steeped in tradition, and as far as I can see, it will take at least another generation before there is any chance of getting the majority of fishing folk sitting on anything that is not made of willow or cane.

After repair

9 ROD RESTS

The more you become involved in match fishing, the more you will realise that a rod rest is not just a thing on which you place your rod while you get out your flask and sandwiches. It is only when there are no prizes or money at stake that you can afford to put down the rod, sit back, and dream away. In pleasure fishing, this idea of putting the rod down and waiting for a possible big fish can be most relaxing, and there is little wonder that in my northern part of the country, rod rests are still referred to as 'idle-backs' – a name that's surely as Yorkshire as a flat cap.

Match angling is also enjoyable, but the rod always has to be near to hand, even if you have gone an hour or so without a bite. You want to be able to pick the rod up and put it down again without having to make sure that the line is not trapped or fouled under the rod rest in any way. A V-ended piece of wood stuck into the river bank may be suitable for some, but for all my match fishing these days, I use only a wide-top rod rest. The best types are those with rubber or plastic-tube 'crossbar'. The wider the rest, the less chance there is of line getting caught up. Many matchmen employ two rod rests when rod-end legering or for swingtipping, but I much prefer to use just a forward rod rest and have my hand firmly on the rod butt. And if I am fishing standing up at a water like the Trent, I simply tuck the rod under my arm when baiting up and taking fish off, using no rod rest at all.

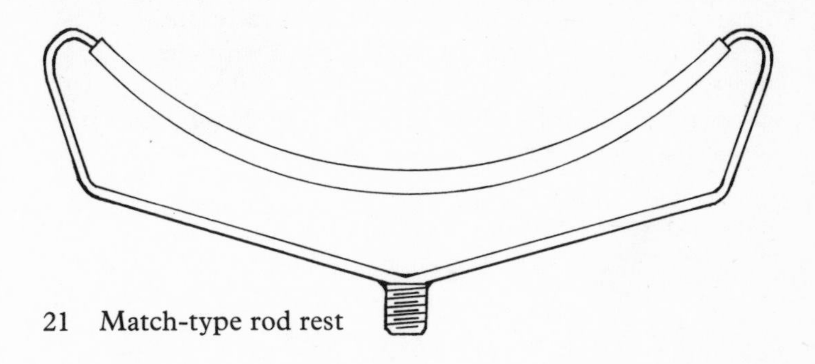

21 Match-type rod rest

It is when swingtipping that I find a wide rod rest most valuable. The rest has to be placed so that the swing-tip is in the most sensitive position. Here again, when a fish gives a bite, you should not have to make sure that the line is not hooked under the rod rest before you strike. It is usually on breezy days that lines are broken on the strike. The wind blows the line round the end of the rest, you strike at a bite, and – twang!

When sitting down 'bleaking' close in, I find that a properly-positioned rod rest is as quick as tucking the rod under an arm. When you are fishing standing up, it is altogether different. The trouble is that on some banks, especially those of concrete or stone, it isn't always possible to fix a bank stick in any useful position. I have heard of men actually using small blocks of concrete with a hole in the middle, but unless you were able to drive up to your peg with a car or van, that idea would not be practical.

More recently, however, some match anglers have been using a clamping device that holds a rod rest bank stick on to the side of a basket. I've not tried the invention myself, although I'm assured it is a great help for matchmen who regularly compete along really hard banks. Incidentally, even on venues where the banks are muddy, it pays to carry a fairly long bank stick for the rod rest. Where a river is deep close in, for example, you may need one 4 feet long or more.

10 SWIM FEEDERS AND BAIT DROPPERS

As far as match angling is concerned, northern men have a reputation for being the first to discover or catch on to new money-winning techniques. It was men from places like Sheffield, Rotherham and Doncaster, for example, who perfected ways of fishing with a swingtip. The title of 'swingtip king' was always bestowed on Yorkshire bream experts who made strange noises on the river bank, such as 'avgoranutha' and 'asthagorowt'. On the roach scene, too, it was Northerners – mostly from Lancashire this time – who first made an impact with the stick float and caster combination.

On the subject of swim feeders and bait droppers however, southern anglers can certainly take credit for being the pioneers. Anglers on the Thames had been catching fish with these for years, long before many northern tackle dealers had found it worthwhile to stock them. Slowly, though, the swim feeder craze has spread north, with huge nets of barbel being taken with these tactics all along the match reaches of the River Severn.

It had to happen on the breamy River Witham sooner or later, and it did in September 1972 when Yorkshireman Alec Lambourne of Garforth, near Leeds, used a swim feeder at Kirkstead to win a big Lincoln Association open event, and take home more than £400. Alec had started a mini-revolution on the Witham, and he couldn't have chosen a better day to do it. The organisers had announced that the winner would receive an added £300 if his weight went over 35 lb. A little lucky, perhaps, Alec's net of bream weighed 35 lb 7½ oz. While he may have been lucky to win an extra £300 with just 7½ ounces to spare, Witham regulars have not forgotten that lesson, and it is for sure that swim feeders and bait droppers of various designs will be more in evidence on that river as years go by. It was realised long ago that heavy groundbaiting is often a mistake for Witham bream, and this is why a swim feeder can be so useful. It can be used to place a few samples of hook bait just in the right spot. Some opponents of swim feeders argue that they lead to an excess of feed being placed into our rivers. I certainly don't agree with that theory. In fact, by being able to groundbait more accurately, it should be possible to use less. And anyway, if a man wants to 'fill his swim in', he will do – swim feeder or no swim feeder.

Some Midland opponents of the swim feeder claim that they cause too much disturbance and can hinder an angler fishing nearby. Another complaint about swim feeders is that they too easily become snagged on river-bed obstacles, leaving yards and yards of broken line trailing in the water. The latter complaint may well be valid, but I don't think it would apply on bream waters such as the Witham, Welland, Great Ouse or Relief Channel, especially in winter.

Incidentally, while we don't hear much about swim feeders being used on Nottinghamshire's River Trent, this method did help Broadwaters matchman Bob Tromans to win on this venue late in 1973. On a day when the river was carrying a lot of extra water, he took about eighty gudgeon on maggot in a contest in the Long Higgin reaches, and won with a weight of 3 lb $4\frac{3}{4}$ oz. I believe that was the first-ever Trent match win by an angler using a swim feeder. I don't think they will ever become popular with the Trent roach anglers, but they could prove useful for men who specialise with chub on this river, especially at match spots such as Holme Marsh and Winthorpe.

I have always felt that swim feeders and bait droppers are most useful in the winter when water temperatures are near to zero. At those times the fish are not so ravenous and it pays to have just a few free samples of hookbait in exactly the right place. If the water is still, it is possible to do this fairly well with a throwing stick or catapult, but when a swim is boily and swirling around, only a swim feeder or bait dropper will guarantee that you are baiting up accurately. That is the advantage of these baiting-up aids. Your hookbait is never far away from the free offerings.

By the way, in matches fished under National Federation of Anglers rules, swim feeders and bait droppers are now allowed. In the past, all groundbait had to be thrown in by hand, but this idea has been scrapped.

There is nothing at all complicated about ordinary open-ended swim feeders. You can buy them from any good tackle shop, or make a few yourself. Many of those in shops are about 3 inches in length, but I prefer them a little smaller. Some of the mass-produced swim feeders hold almost a handful of casters or maggots, far too much for average match fishing. The trouble is that barbel have been known to grab a swim feeder and give a hard but false bite. To make an open-ended feeder, cut out a piece about 2 inches square from a sheet of thin polythene, and drill a series of holes appreciably larger than the bait you are going to use with it. Fold the drilled polythene over, glue it into a cylindrical shape, then add a narrow strip of lead down the glued seam, together with a wire clip and swivel. This type of feeder is particularly useful for bait that does not crawl and wriggle – caster, wasp grub, and hempseed. The general idea is to have the bait in the middle of the feeder and pack both ends solid with fairly stiff bread groundbait. When the bread bait melts, the casters, or whatever you have used, are released onto the river bed. To quicken this up, you can add dry groundbait to the casters, and when this becomes wet it swells up and pushes out the 'plugs'.

The other type of swim feeder is the 'block-end'. As the name implies these are fitted with cups at each end. They come in a variety of shapes, the most useful being cone-shaped, as they do not offer as much resistance in the water. This type is especially suitable for use with maggots, squats and pinkies. Here again, though, it pays to choose one not too big.

Whether you use an open-end or block-end swim feeder, I advise you to fasten it on the line paternoster style, and use it in the same way as you would a string of swan shots or an Arlesey bomb. If you are using a light swim feeder in a strong current, you can, of course, add a bomb or some lead shot to the feeder.

Lastly, we come to the other type of baiting-up device, the bait dropper. In contrast to swim feeders which are often cast quite long distances, the dropper is mostly for using close in. In fact, it is designed to open and release the free offerings when it hits the bottom – after being lowered near or just past the rod end. You can clip it on the terminal tackle to bait up, but I prefer to use a separate rod – with a dropper on only – for putting free offerings on the bottom. When using this idea in matches under N.F.A. rules, remember to take your float tackle out of the water before you use the baiting up rod with a dropper on the end, otherwise you may be disqualified.

The biggest advantage of a bait dropper is, I have found, when normal loose feed is being devoured by masses of surface bleak. Under these circumstances, it can be almost impossible to get some casters or maggots to the big roach on the bottom. But by lowering the free offerings through the bleak, the problem is overcome. You can also use the dropper to put feed 'under your nose' in a fast current.

Whether a swim feeder or bait dropper is used, it is essential to cast accurately to the same spot every time, otherwise you will finish up with small heaps of bait all over the swim, with the fish not knowing if they are coming or going. And it is wise to use a stronger than usual line, dependent on the size of the feeder or dropper. Remember, too, swim feeders and bait droppers do not replace the idea of balls of groundbait or catapulted casters. They are merely alternatives.

11 TACKLE BOX

From what I see on the river banks, there appear to be two distinct kinds of match anglers – those who have everything in its place and a place for everything, and those who lift up the basket lid at the end of every match, pile all the tackle in 'any old how', and leave it like that until the next outing. If you presume that all the top men in our sport are in the first category, you couldn't be more wrong. In fact, some of the men noted for catching match-winning nets of fish are also noted for their disarranged, disorganised way with tackle. They have floats and lead bombs all rattling about together, and on a number of occasions I have seen spare reels put amongst wet groundbait or bankside mud and sand. But still they catch plenty of fish.

Of one thing I am sure. If an expert is organised instead of slap-happy with his tackle, he will catch even bigger nets of fish. In a match it obviously pays if every item is to hand, such as floats, hooks, shots, spare reels and spools. Big contests are so often won and lost by just one fish, and every minute spent searching for a particular hook and float is one minute more of the bait not being in the water. This is the whole essence of being organised – you spend more time actually fishing and less time messing about with tackle. As an added bonus, though, there is less damage to things like floats when they are kept neat and tidy in a proper box.

Personally, I am not in favour of leather-cloth tackle wallets for items such as hooks and floats. They do not offer enough protection when squeezed together with things like maggot tins and keepnets. Also, I do not like the idea of keeping your hooks in a coat pocket. If you do this and leave your coat behind on a hot day, you are in real trouble.

It is best by far to have all your floats in a special float case, with all the other things such as hooks and shots in another box. Or you can have a box divided into spaces to take everything from bite indicators to large floats, right down to dust shots and float rubbers. Whether you have floats in a separate case or not, it pays to keep shots, hooks, weigh scales, Arlesey bombs and other leger weights, spare spools, scissors and forceps in different compartments. My tackle box is made of plywood and I think this is the best material provided you give it a coat of good waterproof paint or varnish. I have found that even though the box may be fitted with a catch to keep the lid closed, it is best to put a fairly strong rubber band around the lot, just to make sure. When you go on matches like the national championships where coach travel is sometimes a condition of entry, fishing baskets have a nasty habit of being turned on their sides, and if that tackle box lid comes undone, you could be in a real mess.

One of the other alternatives to a plywood box is a cantilever-action type made of metal or tough plastic. The smallest of these start at sizes of approximately 14 inches *x* 6 inches *x* 5 inches with two trays, while the larger cantilever tackle boxes go as big as 18 inches *x* 9½ inches *x* 9 inches with four trays. In some of the larger

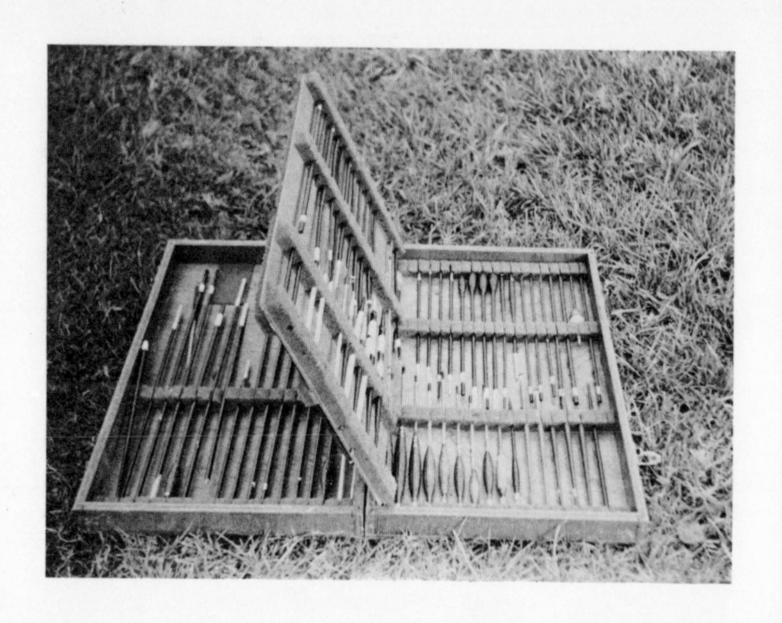

Float case. This latest type is fitted with foam strips

ones, there is room for items like reels in the bottom compartment below the fold-away trays. Perhaps out of tradition, I prefer my tackle boxes home-made out of plywood and exactly the sizes I want. Not only that, a few pieces of plywood and a tube of glue cost far less than a mass-produced container made of metal or plastic.

If you are thinking of getting yourself a separate float case, you can again make one out of plywood, although there are some really excellent ones coming onto the market. The best examples I have seen have the usual top and bottom compartments, and also a hinged centre piece of plywood on which further floats can be clipped. I like particularly those float cases which have strips of foam rubber to hold the floats in position. There are cuts all along the strips of foam, and the floats are simply pushed into them. You can put some of the larger floats in cases of plastic tubing with caps on the ends. But whenever possible, it pays to keep all floats or all the tackle under one lid. That way, there is less chance of any important item going astray.

12 ANGLERS' CLOTHING

Winter match fishing seems to be more popular than ever, and on some stretches of the River Trent, for instance, match pressure is as heavy in December and January as it is in the warmer months of July and August. It could be that today's matchmen are better prepared for cold, wet weather and are less put off by snow showers and freezing winds, or – dare I say it? – are dafter than the match anglers of 20 and 30 years ago. Either way, there are many big winter contests these days, and if you aim to take part in some of them, take my advice and be well prepared to beat the weather. For make no mistake, when conditions are bad, if you don't beat the weather you haven't a chance of beating the bankside opposition either.

As an example, let me tell you of a midwinter match in which I took part quite a few years ago, on the Trent at a spot called Cromwell. Throughout the 5 hour event there was a blinding snowstorm blowing from the east. As we were on the west bank of the river, you can imagine what it was like. In fact when it was all over I found that quite a lot of snow had managed to find its way inside the basket. Anyway, I won that match with 8 lb 14 oz of roach, not because I had drawn the best swim, not because

I was tackled up better or had superior bait to the rest, but simply because I was one of the very few men who was adequately dressed for the shocking weather conditions. Had some of the other anglers been better clad and able to concentrate properly on their fishing, I have no doubt the result sheet could have looked altogether different. Sheffield match angler Bill Eagers was so cold that he never even managed to tie a hook on the line. He tried for a long time to tackle up, but he became colder and colder and finally gave up in desperation. And yet – at that time and on that part of river – he was usually hard to beat.

Yes, when winter is at its worst, the anglers who can keep out the cold stand a much better chance of winning prizes. Anyway, win or lose, there is no fun in sitting on a river bank for 5 hours or so, frozen to the marrow.

One of the main essentials is to keep the feet dry and preferably warm. Where banks are soft, muddy and cold, the best bet is a pair of wellington boots or waders. However, they must be fairly big – roomy enough to enable you to wear an extra pair of sea-boot stockings. As an aid to keeping feet warm, it pays to put your wellington-clad feet in some straw or hay if there is any around. By the way, if you use waders for fishing, don't forget to fasten them up to your belt at the top. And also hang them soles upwards when you arrive home. You can buy clips specially for them. This way, they won't become creased and cracked. For normal from-the-bank match fishing, metal-studded waders are not necessary at all, and the ordinary cleated-sole types are often less expensive.

As far as keeping knees warm is concerned, I have tried all sorts of ideas, but have come to the conclusion that you can't beat an extra-large pair of trousers, with a track-suit bottom-half underneath. An alternative to this is to wear a pair of old-fashioned woolly 'long johns'. If it is wet as well as cold, it is best to cover the whole lot with a pair of waterproof overtrousers. Some of the one-piece suits on the market do a good job of keeping in the warmth and keeping out the cold, but when you have one on, you are apt to look like something that is on its way to the moon.

Before spending a lot of money on a coat, it pays to do a little shopping around. Some of the expensive nylon ones tear easily, and I much prefer an ordinary knee-length coat made of PVC. They are not always available in stout enough material at tackle shops, but I got mine from a marine chandler while on holiday in Devon. Nearer to the skin, I wear a cheap string vest that I got at my local Army and Navy stores, and then a wool coat or some heavy jumpers.

The best piece of modern fishing clothing I have come across in recent years, is a quilted waistcoat made of terylene. It is zipped down the front, has four exceptionally roomy pockets, and is the warmest item of fishing gear – weight for weight – that I have had the pleasure of wearing in the past four winters. These waistcoats, which are specially made for outdoor sports like ours, come in a wide range of sizes and mine is large enough to fit over a sports coat or a number of thick jumpers.

After putting on a woolly scarf to keep the neck warm, all you need then is a hat to keep the head dry, warm, or both. There is an old saying that you should always have warm feet and a cool head. I don't know who invented those few words of wisdom, but I'll bet he wasn't casting a line from a frozen bankside. For most of the season I wear a floppy old Robin Hood type of tatty hat, and I must admit to having some sort of love for it. Nevertheless, when the weather becomes very cold, it is discarded temporarily to make way for a Russian-type fur hat.

It is reckoned that a large proportion of body heat is lost through the head, so that saying 'if you want to get ahead, get a hat' certainly makes sense in match fishing. Handwarmers are ideal for winter pleasure anglers who can afford to sit with hands in pockets, but I doubt their value for matchmen who are busy holding the rod and re-baiting from start to finish. I'm sure it pays, though, to keep a flask of hot soup handy. And another good tip is to have a big hot breakfast not too long before the start of the contest. Mind you, if all else fails, a tot of whisky or rum can work wonders.

13 MISCELLANEOUS TACKLE

UMBRELLAS

I must admit that if I am match fishing standing up and leaning over a river like the Trent, I'll carry on if it pours with rain and not even consider sitting down under an umbrella. I might use a brolly to keep the tackle dry, but that would be all. I would certainly never use one anywhere if it meant that I would catch less fish.

Having said that, I would point out that there are many types of match fishing where an umbrella is no hindrance at all. If you are swingtipping for bream on a fenland-type river, a brolly can be positioned nicely where it will not interfere when you strike at a bite, and can be used to good effect when you are close-in float fishing and are sitting down.

Umbrellas these days are available in sizes of 36 inch rib, 42 inch rib and 45 inch rib. Personally, I think the 36 inch size is too small, the 45 inch too heavy, and the 42 inch just about right. My umbrella is covered with the normal proofed cotton and is quite satisfactory. As an alternative to cotton, brollies are also made in a new laminated vinyl material called 'wavelock'. I haven't tried this new covering myself, but some of my match fishing colleagues assure me that it is absolutely waterproof in the heaviest of rainstorms, and it does not rot. The fact that it is rot-proof should be a boon for those leger men who sometimes use a brolly half submerged in the river to shield a swingtip from the wind.

It is an advantage to have an umbrella with a tilt device built into the pole, but whenever this is used it is advisable to secure the brolly with a pair of guy ropes. The greatest problem with umbrellas – apart from the times when they get in the way – is when the ground is too hard to push in the spike, at a rocky reservoir or stone embankment. I've lost count of the times I've got soaked to the skin simply because I couldn't stick in my brolly. A few years ago, however, I managed to obtain a new device called 'Broltilt' and my hard-ground troubles were over. I don't even know if that invention is still on the market, but I know it has been a success for me and my match fishing.

Fast becoming popular with pleasure anglers and specimen hunters are the latest fishing shelters. The trouble is, though, that most I have seen have been too small for the average match angler who wishes to have his tackle box and a variety of baits around him. And in a facing wind, you will certainly get your knees wet.

BITE INDICATORS

While the swingtip is generally the best type of bite indicator when you are legering far-off in matches, there are times when a bite indicator – clipped onto the butt section of the rod – is far better. I am thinking about those days when there are high waves on the water and you want to sink all of the line well under, from bomb to rod tip. In fact it was like that when I got my biggest-ever national net of 26 lb 15 oz on the Huntspill River in Somerset. I used a clip-on bite indicator that day.

The indicator I use most is very similar to the cane swingtip I explained in an earlier chapter, except that it has only one runner on. In this case, however, the short section of rubber tube is connected to an ordinary Terry clip. It is best to have a variety of clips made up with pieces of tube fastened on. This way you can use a bite indicator, no matter what diameter the rod butt is. The best way is to have a ring clasp (as on a necklace) on the end of the indicator, allowing the indicator to be brought into action – or taken out – without disturbing the terminal rig. When using an indicator of this type, it is essential to point the rod straight down the line. I prefer to carry a selection of different-weight indicators to suit the various flows.

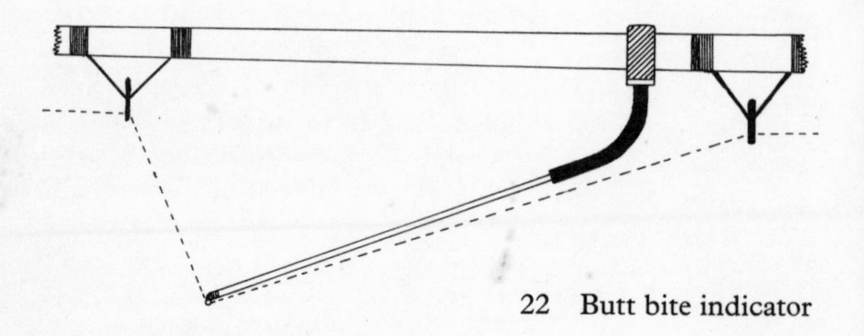

22 Butt bite indicator

ROD HOLDALLS

Nothing is worse than leaving a rod at home simply because there isn't enough room for it in the holdall. Usually two or three rods are ample, but there are times when a bigger assortment is needed. Apart from the width of the holdall, it is best to pick one that is long enough and with a few inches to spare. Always choose one, too,

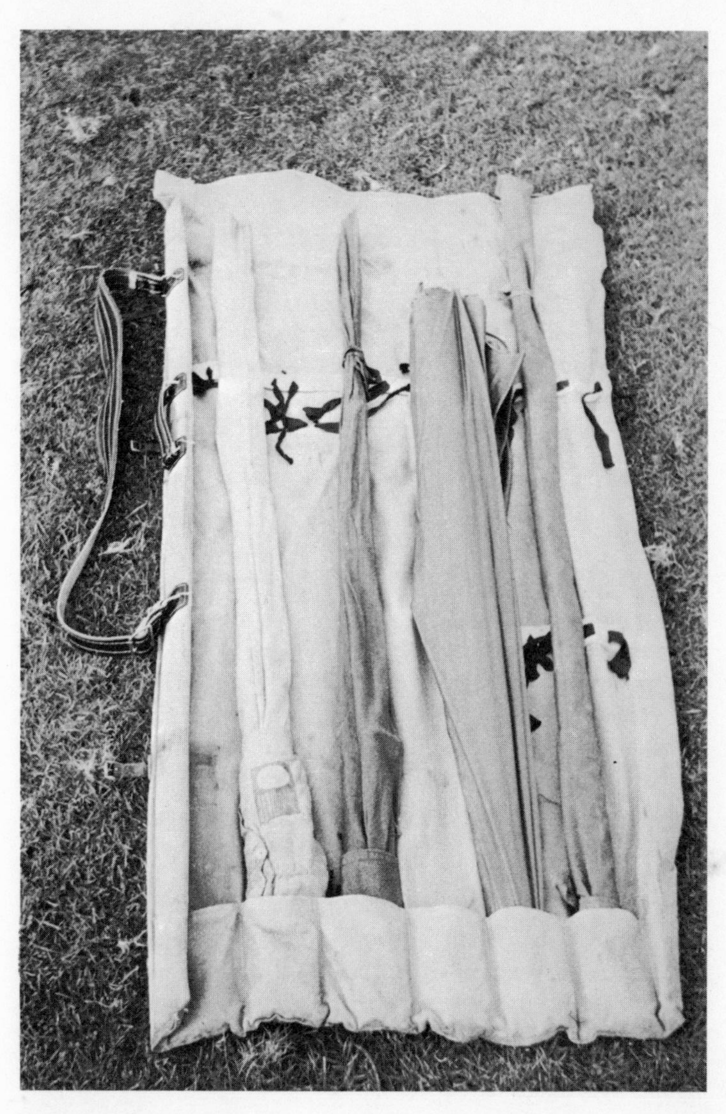

Roll-up rod holdall

that has a stiffener down one edge, and I would always make sure that it has metal studs in the bottom. It is desirable to have a holdall with at least three pockets – for rods, umbrella and rod rests. To help the bottom of the inside of the holdall to dry out after wet rods have been in it, I have drilled about a dozen $\frac{1}{4}$ inch holes in the studded leather base of mine.

The next thing I have promised myself is a roll-up rod holdall. With these, there is no chance of rod runners being broken when you are putting the rods away. The space in them is almost unlimited, but like all other items of tackle, the bigger they are, the heavier they are. And weight does matter. After all, it is you who have to carry it.

TACKLE TROLLEY

I have had a tackle trolley ever since they first became really popular, and I must say it has been a tremendous asset on waters like the Relief Channel in Norfolk where walks between bridges can be most exhausting. You just fasten the basket and bait bag on the trolley, lie the rods across the handle, and you are away to your peg in next to no time. Of course, if the banks are muddy it will be more difficult, and when there are quite a number of fences or stiles to climb over, it can actually be a handicap. Otherwise, when there is a long walk along a clear bank it can save you doing yourself an injury.

A word of warning about the use of tackle trolleys. Sheffield matchman Keith Boswell was using a trolley and it nearly cost him one eye. He was securing the basket on to the trolley with one of those big elastics with hooks on the ends, and – wham! His elastic slipped at the other end. So be warned.

TARGET BOARD

While one of the main essentials in match fishing is to get bites, those bites are no use at all if you do not detect them. In a nutshell, that is why target boards have become so popular amongst match anglers who leger regularly using a swingtip or quiver-tip. It is along still-waters where the target board is of most value. On running waters you usually get a bite that you cannot fail to see, board or no board. A great advantage when you have a target board is that you can use it to shield a swingtip or quiver-tip from the wind. The idea with a swingtip is to use a board with a clear perspex window in it, and have the tip out of the wind. It pays to put a series of marks on the target board as you spot bites better this way. Obviously you will have the wind in your back when swingtipping, but when using a quiver-tip, it pays to face the wind and have the tip almost touching the board. Even today, however, there is still much controversy about target boards, and it is true that some of the best swingtippers in the business have never yet found use for one.

WEED DRAG

On two big match waters in particular, the Witham and Welland, a wide fringe of marginal weed growth provides large problems every summer. The trouble is in some swims, if you do manage to get the big bream feeding, it isn't so easy to get them out. Down on the south-west parts of the country, match anglers on the King's Sedgemoor Drain are often confronted by heavy weed, and there are scores of other waters – wide canals especially – where a weed drag of some kind will increase your chance of success.

Obviously if you are going to concentrate on roach

one or two rod lengths out from the bank, a fringe of weed would actually be an asset. Certainly in those circumstances it would be suicide to disturb the weed and fish in any way. But it is a different story when you are swingtipping or float fishing far off for bream. Where the bream are hooked, the river may be fairly weed-free, but when playing the fish towards the landing net, there can be real trouble if there is 15 or 20 feet, and more, of growth. In this type of situation it pays to get the fish to the top of the water as soon as possible, stand up from the bank, and try to skate it over the weed.

However, the best way is to clear a patch through the weed. If it doesn't go much more than 10 or 12 feet from the bank, a weed drag fastened to the end of a pole is best. On the other hand, I am often faced with much more weed, and I prefer to carry a drag and rope in the bottom of my basket. This way I can clear a channel through the weed, whether it be 10, 15 or even 20 feet wide. My drag is simply an anchor-shaped piece of steel, and it fits nice and flat in the basket. If you fish regularly on a venue where you can drive to the waterside or don't have to walk far, a heavier object such as a pair of garden rake heads, tied together, would do the job quicker. Remember, though, to keep the splashings down to a minimum, especially on a water that is not very wide.

CATAPULT AND THROWING STICK

It's a few years since the N.F.A. dropped their match ban on bait-throwing aids like catapults and throwing sticks, and most top matchmen now regard at least one of these as part of their general equipment. When it comes to throwing loose feed such as casters or maggots, a catapult especially will make it easier and also far more accurate. Some men use catapults to send balls of groundbait across a river, but I use mine mostly for putting a dozen or so maggots or casters just in the right spot.

While you may need the cup on a catapult as much as 3 inches across for balls of groundbait, one half this size is ample for loose feed. Some of the latest ones have circular frames and three or four elastics. But I am still using a U-shaped catapult with the usual two elastics and find it quite satisfactory. I think it is important to have the elastics the right length and strength. Mine are just over 1 foot long and $\frac{1}{8}$ inch diameter. I have tried catapults fitted with soft pouches instead of a rubber cup, but I find that maggots and casters tend to get trapped in them at times.

A big open water such as Rudyard Lake in Staffordshire is the only type of venue where I use a catapult for sending out balls of groundbait. On these places, it is sometimes best to throw groundbait as far as you can, then send a leger weight and baited hook to the same spot. On waters only 20 and 30 yards wide, though, I just throw cereal bait in by hand. Whichever way you choose, it has to be accurate, and I find it best to pick a target on the opposite bank and send some bait along the same path every time. The only thing you have to bother about then is the distance.

As opposed to catapults which can throw maggots and casters a tremendous distance in favourable conditions, the throwing stick is more useful for loose feeding far-bank swims on fairly narrow waters such as canals. All you need is about 2 feet of bamboo cane or hollow fibreglass, a little less than an inch in diameter. To form a cup in one end, insert a cork and glue it in place about 2 inches down. That's it finished. You simply put some bait in the cupped end, and give a quick flick of the arm or wrist. You can use it for maggots, casters, and hemp, but I find it particularly useful when free-offering with pinkies and squats. Naturally, if you are fishing close in, it is much quicker to dip your hand into the maggots and throw a few in. As you may have found, however, the fish are not always 'under your nose'.

Other accessories you will need are: a set of maggot cartons of various sizes; a large bowl for mixing cereal groundbait; a canvas bucket for carrying dry groundbait; a bait stand with clips for holding maggot cartons; a small spring balance to weigh your catch on practice sessions; a pair of artery forceps and two or three disgorgers; and other odds and ends such as a maggot bag to hang round your neck, a towel, and a few tiny swivels.

Bait stand

Part Two

BAITS

Remembering that most fishing waters hold a good supply of natural food, and taking into account the vast quantities of bread, maggots, casters and hempseed that are thrown in by anglers, it isn't at all surprising that the fish – especially in heavily-fished match waters – are choosy about what they eat. They can afford to be. After all, they are not going to stay in front of you all day and eat your tough maggots and your sour casters, if the men either side are feeding with gozzers and freshly-turned casters. In match fishing, this is a most important lesson. If you do not give or offer them top-class bait, some other competitor will. Of course, the trouble is that the baits passed over the tackle shop counters seem to get dearer as each year goes by, and there is no doubt that the cost of entering twenty or thirty matches in a season is far more expensive than it used to be. Nevertheless, compared to a go-it-alone pleasure-only man or specimen hunter, the competition man does stand to get more than pleasure in return. Indeed, after investing money in a few pints of casters and maggots, there are no complaints if you are lucky enough to have a bundle of pound notes stuffed into your smelly hands at the finish. Apart from money, the top men in match angling often spend hours and hours preparing, breeding and making sure their baits are second to none. It is no use complaining after a match that your baits were lacking in quantity or quality. Prizes are presented for the biggest nets of fish, and – if you are to stand a chance of showing a profit – you have to take enough of the right baits to catch the fish.

The thing to do, of course, is to decide which baits, and in what quantity, you will require for the match in question. For instance, if you were preparing for a summer match outing to a roach venue, it might well be that a few handfuls of hempseed and tares would offer the most chance of success. And yet, if it was winter, with bream the main quarry, the priority bait could be worm or casters. Having decided on the bait, make sure it is as good as you can get it, and also ensure you are not going to run out halfway through the match. Naturally, we all make a wrong choice of baits now and again – and we certainly cannot afford to take them all – but if you choose the right ones on most days and present them properly to suit the conditions, you should pick up a prize or two now and then.

If you take my advice and prepare or collect your own baits whenever possible, a refrigerator – or permission to use the family one – is essential. For instance, if you come home from one match with three pints of maggots, you can pop them in the fridge for a day or two, then bring them back out at the right time to turn them into casters for the following match. For other baits such as squats, pinkies and wasp grubs, a second-hand family-type fridge can more than pay for itself in a busy match season. There are odd weekends when squats, pinkies, and even maggots are in short supply, especially in the busy parts of the summer, and for this reason alone it pays to keep a few 'on ice'. Conversely, a wasp grub expert with a fridge can be using this bait long after all the wasps have gone to ground for the winter. Unused luncheon meat can be saved in the same way. I just pop the meat into an airtight bag, and it is then kept in the fridge until the next match or practice session on a chub or barbel venue.

Fridge or no fridge, you want to go to a match with enough of the right baits for that particular venue, yet at the same time not be lumbered with a lot of stuff that is likely to be of no use. Past experiences, and references to your match diary or log book, should help you decide which waters call for which baits. On the other hand, if you are to compete on a strange venue – and this is certainly not the best way to win money – you may simply have to keep your ear to the ground and carry a few reserve baits. Having first decided which baits are most likely to put you on the money trail, here in the following pages are the best ways to prepare them.

14 MAGGOTS

Since my early fishing days, maggots – the larvae of the bluebottle fly – have been the most popular bait among coarse anglers, and it is still the same today. In fact the greatest problem in the peak match periods is that many tackle shops are unable to get enough to meet demand. And yet most maggot farms in this country are working to full capacity, and one in particular turns out 3,500 gallons a week and is having to turn some tackle dealers away. At the maggot farms, the maggots are fed on such things as dead chickens, turkeys, sheep, calves and pigs. Fish offal is also used when obtainable. When the maggots have reached maturity, they are stored in vast refrigerators, then distributed to dealers in various parts of the country, sometimes in large vans fitted with refrigeration units.

If the breeder has done his job properly, and the tackle dealer in turn has kept the maggots cold, there should still be plenty of feed (dark patches of food) in them when they are handed over the counter. If there are no feed marks at all, your so-called fresh maggots could all be chrysalises less than two days later. Provided that the maggots are fresh and full of feed, you should be able to rely on them for up to at least five days, more if the weather is really cold. Apart from being able to keep them longer without their turning, fresh maggots are the softest and a 'must' for the match angler. If you are persistently being sold old tough maggots, it's time you found another dealer, preferably one who fishes himself and knows what you are talking about. Another thing, when buying, say, 3 pints of maggots, make sure that is what you are getting. Sawdust has to be put with maggots to stop them becoming overheated, but when you buy them, make sure the maggots are measured out first, and then the sawdust added – not vice versa. A few years ago, a national angling newspaper carried out a survey on tackle shops all over the country. The results from one area to another varied enormously. In my home city of Sheffield, for instance, if you asked for a pint of maggots, you got exactly that. And yet over the Pennines in Manchester, the survey proved that one shop was serving $\frac{1}{2}$ pint of sawdust and $\frac{5}{8}$ pint of maggots – more than a pint altogether, but still short measure. Certainly maggots have to be kept in sawdust by the tackle dealer, but the angler should not have to pay for the sawdust. It should be riddled off before the maggots are measured out.

One pleasing trend, however, is that you can usually choose between yellows, whites and anattoes, far better than in the days when maggots every colour of the rainbow were mixed together. If I want coloured maggots, I prefer to buy them as whites and dye them myself.

I think the best colour is yellow, and this is how I dye them by using chrysodine. Having bought, say, 2 pints of white maggots, riddle away the sawdust or bran if any has been added, and then give them a few drops of chrysodine in liquid form. Give the maggots a good shake and finally put them into bran or dry bread groundbait. If you haven't already got any liquid dye, it is quite easy to prepare. The best way is to purchase an ounce of chrysodine powder (some fishing tackle dealers stock it, and it can also be obtained occasionally at chemist shops), and put it into an empty 1 pint tin can. Half fill the can with water, bring to the boil, and simmer for about 10 to 15 minutes. After that, allow the rich-coloured dye to cool, pour it into a lemonade-sized bottle, and top up with cold water. This large bottle of dye should be enough for a number of fishing seasons. Using chrysodine in powder form, most anglers make a right mess of things when it comes to the job of colouring a cartonful of maggots. Their hands become stained all over, and many a wife has had good reason to complain about a big red patch on the living room carpet. In fact, the only things some anglers don't manage to colour properly are the maggots themselves. Try it my way, and you will have no trouble.

By the way, whether your maggots are yellow, or even red white and blue, never cram too many together. The usual-size cartons are all right for a pint or a little more, though when storing – or taking to the waterside – bigger amounts, biscuit tins are the best. Unless the maggots are in a fridge, however, never put more than 4 pints together in one biscuit tin, or they will overheat and 'stretch', as it is known in the trade. Ordinary maggots need air to live, so it is best to use a lid with plenty of holes, or, better still, use no lid at all. At the waterside, many northern anglers from places such as Leeds and York have maggots hung in a bag around their necks. This idea is best when you are fishing standing up in an awkward spot. When fishing standing up on a roomy piece of bank, though, I much prefer to have maggots in tins or cartons, using the basket top as a bait table. Another tip is to use wide shallow maggot containers instead of tall narrow ones. Besides helping to keep maggots cool, they enable you to pick one, two, or even a handful out more easily.

Incidentally, if you bring maggots home from one

match to keep in a fridge until the following week, or fridge maggots for any other reason, never allow the temperature of the fridge to drop below zero. Otherwise, there is a good chance that some will die. Also, if I am keeping maggots of any kind for more than a day in a fridge, I always use sawdust, not bran or groundbait. A big problem, of course, is when you are away from home on a 5 or 6-day trip in the middle of summer. Normally, most of the maggots would be turning to chrysalises before it was time to come home, but I have a way of at least slowing up the turning process. I find a shady spot under some trees, dig a hole about 18 inches deep, and then put a carton of maggots in, with a lid on. Before piling the earth back on top of the maggots, put some dock leaves or other large leaves over the lid to ensure that the holes in the lid do not become blocked. You can use this method at home if you haven't the use of a fridge.

In the middle of winter, tough-skinned maggots tend to wriggle and keep alive longer than tender ones. But in summer – especially on hard-fished bream venues – it certainly pays to offer the fish a maggot as soft as possible. There is only one way to ensure a steady supply of soft maggots, gozzers, specials, or anything else you want to call them, and that is to breed them yourself. It isn't all that much trouble, and can put you in touch with match-winning fish when otherwise you might not even have known that they were around. Breeding maggots is not a thing you are likely to do just right first time, so if you have never tried it my way before, it would pay to have a 'dummy run' or two in the weeks leading up to the start of the match season.

Anyway, this is how I get really special maggots, much softer than you will ever buy over a tackle shop counter. First of all, you have to get some bluebottle blows (eggs that they lay in small white clusters). In a quiet corner of the garden or allotment, arrange a 'blowing box', a biscuit tin or something similar with holes large enough in the lid to allow a fairly big fly to crawl in. Next, you have to get something 'meaty' for the bluebottles to lay their eggs on. The best thing for obtaining blows quickly is a fresh chicken head. When the chicken head has been put on some paper in the tin, put on the lid, and shield from rain and direct sunlight with a sloping piece of board.

Having got enough blows, which should take little more than a day in warm dry weather, take the chicken head out of the blowing box, and add to it whatever you want your maggots to feed on. Personally, I think there is nothing to beat pigs' or sheeps' hearts. To obtain enough maggots for a big match on a bream water, you will need at least two of these hearts, especially if they are rather small. If hearts of pig or sheep are not available, you can use cows' heart, chicken, fish or rabbit. Pigeon maggots are also good, and these have widely become known as gozzers. The next thing is to wrap up the hearts, pigeon, or whatever you have chosen, with the blown chicken head. Keep wrapping it up in newspaper or in other paper as they do with fish and chips. You will need about eight or nine sheets. Then put the whole parcel away in a dry spot where other flies – and cats and dogs – cannot get at it.

After about four days, open the parcel, and have a look to see if all is well. By this time there should be hundreds of maggots, tiny ones, all nibbling away. If it seems that the food supply is likely to run out, simply add some more heart or chicken. At this stage in the breeding operation, you can also add some colouring agent so that the maggots will, as they say in match fishing, be 'colour-fed'. If you prefer chrysodine maggots, it is best to colour them after they have become fully grown, as described earlier. But if you want your maggots coloured a butter

Maggots. For summer bream especially, it pays to breed your own

colour with anatto roll, it has to be mixed with a drop of water and made into a smooth paste, and added to the maggots halfway through the feeding period. The maggots don't actually like eating anatto, so you have to put it on the feed when they are about half grown and more ravenous than ever. I have mentioned anatto maggots, not because they are always better than whiter-than-white ones, but simply because there are days when the fish prefer them. It may even pay to double the breeding operation – one of all-whites, and one with added anatto. I sometimes add brown sugar at the halfway stage, but to be quite honest, I am not at all sure whether it makes the maggots more acceptable. I do know that it attracts wasps to your fingers on the river bank!

Anyway, whether you have added colouring, sugar, or anything else, wrap up the parcel again, and leave it for two or three days, dependent, of course, on the weather.

In a really cool spell, the whole operation will take several days longer than in a warm one. It helps, though, to add more paper wrapping when the weather is not so hot.

When the maggots are fully grown and have devoured all the food, put them in a clean plastic maggot container, with some fine sawdust that has been dampened. Left like this for a day or so, the special maggots would be in peak condition for use as hookbait and free offerings. But if the breeding has gone along quicker than expected, you can keep them in the fridge. Again I remind you, though, not to freeze them to death.

As always in our world of angling, there are exceptions to the rule, and while it pays to use soft maggots for shy bream and roach in heavily-fished match waters, it is a different story altogether as far as bleak are concerned. With these tiny fish, it is an aid to speed if you can catch

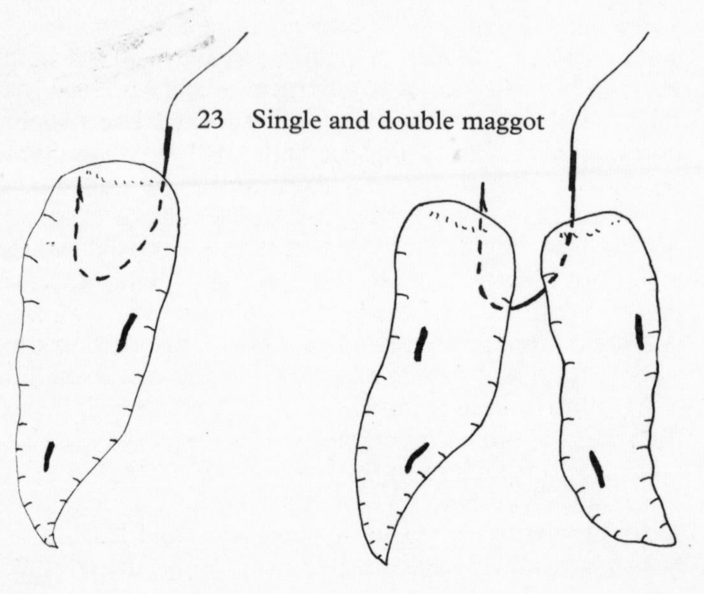

23 Single and double maggot

four, five or six and more on the same maggot, and it is an obvious advantage – in these circumstances – to have a fairly tough maggot (about two-thirds grown) that has been kept in dry coarse sawdust for several days.

The main thing in all kinds of fishing is to present a bait in such a manner that will bring a bite. And as far as maggot is concerned, I am convinced that when using this bait singly, it pays to leave the point of the hook inside. In theory, this may seem to be all against hook penetration, but at the waterside, with cups and money at stake, I have found that I get more than my share of bites, and don't have more than my share of missed ones.

Of course, we often need more than one maggot on a hook, especially for some of the bigger species, and I have won hundreds of pounds in some contests while baiting with two and three at a time. Going to the extreme, it occasionally pays dividends really to fill a big hook with maggots. For instance, I remember one November day in 1973, when Midlands matchman Martin Folkes won a Birmingham AA welfare match on the River Severn at Quatford. On that match day, he needed just two big barbel for a fairly low weight of 7 lb 14 oz, but he tempted them with 14 maggots on a size 4 hook!

15 SQUATS

Squats are the larvae of the common house fly, and it is not practical for the average matchman to breed them. If there is any complaint to be made about squats, it is that they are sometimes not available during the match season in many parts of the country. It is a pity really, because when maggot is the hookbait for bream, roach, perch and all kinds of other species, squats are the best things to attract those fish into your swim and keep them there. The idea is to have a carpet of these tiny maggots on the river bed, then offer something a bit bigger, such as a gozzer, on the hook. Now and again, of course, the fish become so pre-occupied with squats, that it pays to use the squats on the hook, in ones, twos and threes. Alternatively, I've sometimes done well with bream while using two big maggots tipped with just one squat on the point of the hook.

When using squats on bream waters such as the Great Ouse, River Witham or the Welland, they have to be introduced with bread groundbait to get them to the desired spot. Even if you could throw squats well out at a bream water, they would most likely be taken away by the current, or be gobbled up by surface-feeding species such as bleak.

Mind you, whenever bleak offer a winning chance, squats – loose fed – can maintain the feeding frenzy of these tiny fish. In this case, it is actually an advantage that they sink slowly. And to make sure that the hookbait squat sinks as slowly as the free offerings, it pays to use a tiny hook such as a number 22. I would use squats as an attraction for bleak in the colder months, but in the wintry weather I rarely add them to cereal bait for bream, as they soon die in icy water.

Going back many years, our match-angling forefathers used to have to scrape around in manure to find a few squats. But now they are bred commercially and are usually sold to matchmen by the gallon or half-gallon. Mostly, squats are bred on maggot farms in the north of England. Consequently, especially at the busiest times of the year, the southern men sometimes have difficulty in getting hold of this bait. By the way, squats are usually sold in damp sand, and it is best to keep them that way. If the squats appear to be fresh with plenty of feed still in them, I always fatten them further by giving them a slice of bread soaked in milk. Whether you feed them or not, it is important to keep them in a wide open tin. Never put the lid on, or they will sweat and escape through the holes. As with maggots, you can store them in a fridge. With squats, however, it is most important to keep the fridge temperature at least one or two degrees above zero.

16 PINKIES

Pinkies, the larvae of the greenbottle, are altogether different from squats or ordinary bluebottle maggots. And first and foremost, you must remember that they can crawl out of any maggot carton or biscuit tin if the lid is left off. Many a newcomer to our sport has got up on the morning of a match, only to find that all his pinkies have 'done a moonlight', perhaps never to be seen again. With a lid on, however, they are easy to keep, and I've had them up to two months with the refrigerator set to around freezing point. They are best kept in either sawdust, bread groundbait (dry), or maize meal.

As with bluebottle maggots, pinkies can be bred by the match angler. The important thing, of course, is to make sure you get the right type of blows. One of the best ways is to pick up a dead rabbit or hare which has been killed on the road a day or two earlier. If it has been blown in broad daylight, you can usually rely on greenbottles being responsible. Sometimes you might be lucky and find a carcase which is already crawling with pinkies. It is a messy business sometimes, but the rewards can make it all worthwhile. By the way, just as fish sometimes prefer ordinary maggots coloured, they often bite faster on pinkies when they are yellow instead of a natural colour. A number of big contests have been won by anglers using anatto pinkies for bream.

Pinkies are an excellent bait when catching roach, dace and bleak 'on the drop', and are used for bream in the same way as squats. The trouble is, though, pinkies are a strong type of maggot and can easily break up a ball of bread groundbait. For bream, I use them double and treble on a size 18 or 16 hook, while for smaller species I use them singly on a size 20 or 22.

17 CASTERS

Having decided that casters – maggot chrysalises – are so very often an essential match fishing bait, you are left with a choice of two things – paying a high price over the tackle shop counter, or spending a little time and trouble preparing your own. There are many anglers who complain of the current price of shop casters, and they are quick to point out that whereas maggot chrysalises were once considered as waste matter in the fishing tackle trade, dealers are now cashing in on demand and selling them at a much higher price than maggots. On the other hand, there are many dealers who grumble that despite the shop prices, casters are more trouble than they are worth. Indeed, in a busy tackle shop, the problem of producing gallons of first-class casters is almost a full-time job for somebody. It all depends, of course, how well organised the tackle dealer is. And while some dealers actually dislike the demand for casters – and often haven't any on sale – other tackle shops have gallons on hand and have never had things so good until the caster craze started.

Whether your local tackle man makes a loss or a living out of casters, they remain an expensive match fishing item. The truth is, however, no matter where you go

A match-winning pike. Yorkshire's Dave Smith clutches the 20¾-pounder that took his single caster bait and gave him top prize in an Angling Telegraph Championship Match (*by courtesy of Angling Telegraph*)

coarse fishing these days, you can hardly afford to be without a pint or two of this deadly bait. Wherever match anglers compete, casters seem to pick out the better-class fish of each species – roach on the Trent, bream on the Witham, chub on the Severn and Wye, and barbel on the Yorkshire Ouse, just to mention a few.

There have been a tremendous number of match wins on caster, but the most amazing I can remember was when Yorkshireman Dave Smith of Conisbrough took top prize in the 1973 Angling Telegraph Championships on the River Witham at Kirkstead. Using a size 16 hook baited with a single caster on swingtip tackle, he landed the match-winning fish to beat them all – a pike of 20 lb 12 oz hooked in the bottom lip!

In that same year, by the way, Lincolnshire matchman Ken Taylor hauled out 51 lb 2 oz to win the Boston AA Clayton and Pearson event on the Witham. On that day, he used worm on the hook, but attracted the big bream by mashing casters in his groundbait. A theory held by some Lincolnshire matchmen is that if you throw pulped-up casters into your swim, the fish smell the juice and are encouraged to come bang on feed. Judging from that catch on the Witham, I reckon they could be right.

Away from the fenlands of Lincolnshire, though, it has frequently been proved that casters are a bait which you cannot afford to miss out. Up in Yorkshire, for instance, Leeds match angler George Hartley won a York AA Hospital Cup competition on the Yorkshire Ouse with 71 lb 5 oz of bream and barbel taken on a number 8 hook filled with casters.

Going back to 1972, casters (two on a size 14 hook) were the bait when match ace Bob Tromans won the River Wye Championships with a 63 lb 6 oz net of chub. The real proof of the power of the caster came a year later, when Coventry man Arthur Williams used this bait to win a club match on the Great Ouse with a bream net weighing 94 lb 11¾ oz – a match record for that river.

Although you may be convinced that casters are so often a number one bait, the aim nevertheless should be to get them of the highest quality and as cheaply as possible. As you will probably have found out, maggots in a tackle shop cost quite a lot less than casters, so the obvious thing to do is to buy maggots and turn them into casters yourself. Of course, now and again we are caught on the hop when somebody comes round and says the inevitable: 'Going fishing?' You drop everything and before you can say: 'Give me a hand to put the tackle in the van', the trip is on and there is a 'Gone fishing' note left for your wife. On those days – and there are plenty of them for me – there is sometimes no other choice but to buy a bag or two of casters on the journey out of town.

It is far better, though, to get maggots well in advance, and produce your own casters. It isn't all that much trouble, and these days I sometimes have a pint or two of fresh ones in the fridge, even when there isn't a match. So, if like me you have decided casters are worthwhile, here is how to produce your own. First of all, forget all that talk of picking casters out of maggots every night and then putting them into water. Just imagine picking out two or three pints of casters, one by one.

My way is far simpler. Having decided that, say, 2½ pints of casters are needed for a match outing one weekend, buy 3 pints of big fresh maggots (preferably yellow ones) about a week before the planned trip. If you go fishing every weekend, it would pay to collect a few pints of maggots every Saturday and use them as casters the following weekend, and so on. After picking up the maggots from the tackle shop, mix them with plenty of fine sawdust. Whatever you do, don't put them in bran, as it sticks to the casters and they become less attractive to fish.

Having purchased fresh maggots on Saturday, and then kept them in a fairly moderate temperature – in an outhouse in summer, or perhaps in the house in icy weather – they should still be pretty lively by the following Tuesday or Wednesday.

But by the Thursday, things should be starting to happen, and there should be at least a few maggots turning to casters. At this stage, the sawdust must be riddled off. Then empty all the maggots onto a riddle with holes that will just allow maggots to crawl through and drop into a container underneath – I use a baby's bathtub. When all the maggots have made their way through the mesh of the riddle, pick off the dead maggots (if there are any) and throw them away.

The casters on the riddle must then be put into a fairly small plastic bag, the neck of it made airtight, and then

Casters on riddle

Trent roach. The author with 45 lb taken in five hours using casters

placed in the fridge (a few degrees above freezing). As often as is convenient, repeat the riddling operation, and add the casters to those in the plastic bag. By the Saturday following the weekend you bought the maggots, you should have all casters and no maggots. Ideally, the casters should be orange in colour. The time of year and the temperature will dictate the timing of the whole operation, but by moving the maggots to a warmer place, or a warmer part of the house, you can speed things up a little, and vice versa. While the whole plan is aimed at producing casters, otherwise called 'sinking chrysalis', it sometimes pays to keep, say, half a handful of them out of the fridge where they will eventually turn to floaters. These can be useful as hookbait, especially when used in conjunction with the sinking free offerings.

It sounds easy, my caster production method, and it is, but there are a few points to remember. Most important, the maggots must be out of the same batch (all of the same age); casters should always be as fresh as possible; and only put the casters into water to stop them turning to floaters if you haven't the use of a fridge.

When going to a match, it pays to carry the casters in separate $\frac{1}{2}$-pint or 1-pint plastic bags. And then by using and finishing one bag at a time, your casters are as good as they can be. Usually you want big casters, and that is why it is so important to buy big maggots to produce them. With a good caster, you should be able to bury a size 14 hook, although it is sometimes necessary to scale things down to a number 16 or 18 for roach as shy as those on the Trent.

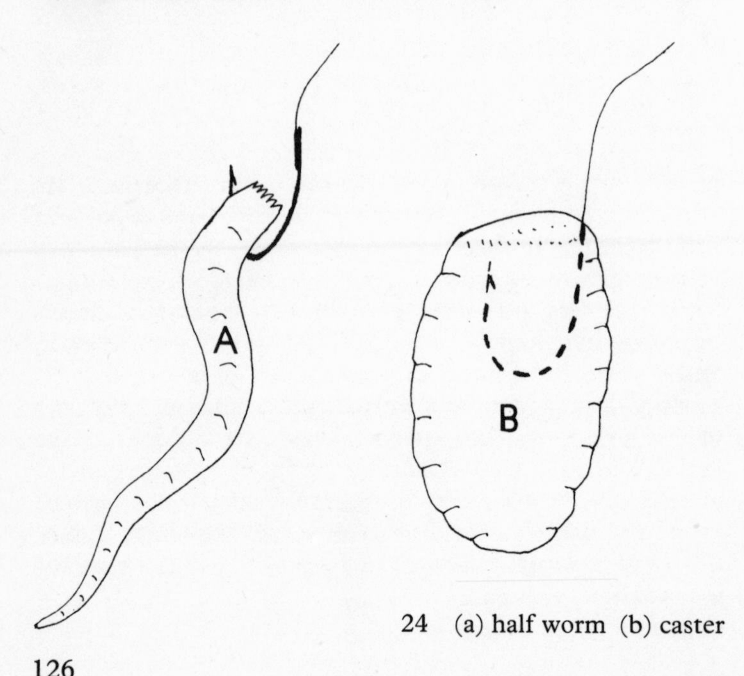

24 (a) half worm (b) caster

18 BRANDLINGS

Brandlings are small red worms with yellow hoops around their bodies, and are often found in animal manure heaps. If your match programme is to include events on bream waters from September and into the winter, brandlings will have to be on your bait list. In fact, for that species at that time of year, it is my number one bait. And given an extra foot or so of floodwater, brandlings become even more deadly. A pleasing thing is that they tend to sort out the bigger bream, and, at the same time, you often get a really good bite. Target boards can be useful for a man catching summer bream on maggot, but I've never yet come across bream in winter that gave shy bites on worm. Come to that, I've had bream grabbing a brandling and pulling the rod right round on a flowing river.

Occasionally, I float-fish with brandlings if perch are the quarry, but for bream I always use them on leger tackle, in conjunction with a swingtip or quiver-tip. Typical rivers where I use the leger and worm combination in winter are the Welland, Nene, Witham and Great Ouse. Brandlings fished on the bottom also account for bream on stillwaters, although under these conditions it usually pays to twitch them towards you, a bit at a time.

I think it makes the worm appear to be more alive, but whatever the reason, it certainly brings more bites. When brandlings are the bait – for any species – I always fish them in halves. When broken, the yellow juice runs out and smells terrible, but this, I am sure, helps the fish to find them. With half a brandling as bait, the best hook sizes are 16 and 14. This leaves quite a lot of hook showing, although the bream in winter don't seem to mind this at all. Certainly it is a waste of time threading a worm on the line, as some of the old angling books advise.

When worming for bream, it helps if you chop up some worms and add them to a cereal groundbait. Obviously, if a river is flowing strongly, the bait will have to be heavy enough to put those free offerings in just the right spot. Surprisingly, even when worm is on the hook, casters in the groundbait can be just as vital as chopped worms. In fact in winter on some bream waters, a worm (or piece of one) on the hook with casters in the groundbait is the most likely way to a top prize.

The best way with brandlings is to collect them and bag them up before the cold weather arrives. At the start of every winter I always have a good supply, all in damp peat and in small airtight plastic bags. If you did this with maggots, they would soon die, but airtight worms will last for several months. By the way, it is much better to use a good supply of small bags rather than one large one. This way, if something goes wrong in one bag, you have plenty of others left in reserve. It is important, too, to keep the worms neither too hot nor too cold. They should certainly not be placed in a fridge, or where frost can reach them.

Brandling, with their red bodies and yellow hoops, are easy to recognise, and you can usually find some in a well-established animal manure heap. Pig manure is usually a sure spot for brandlings, but it pays to dig around in the heap of manure until you find a place where they are really concentrated. It is a smelly business, to say the least, but if you collect plenty in, say, late September and bag them properly, you should have enough for a winter of breaming. Digging on a pig farm for worms can vastly improve your chances of winning in matches, although I wouldn't like to do it many times a year.

A more pleasant way with brandlings and other small red worms is to build your own worm heap with alternate layers of earth and rotting vegetables such as grass cuttings, leaves and cabbage stalks. An old rug or some sacks put over it helps, and it is essential to keep the whole lot damp. Whatever you do, don't use grass cuttings from a lawn that has been treated with weed-killer. You can add some worms to the heap at the start, although you will find that if the heap suits the worms, they will soon begin to show up even without an initial stock. On the other hand, if the heap is not 'ripe' enough for their liking, they will not stay, no matter how many worms you put in.

19 LOBWORMS

Lobworms are those big fat juicy worms we often find in the garden, 4, 5 and sometimes 6 inches in length. For the average match angler there is never any reason to try breeding lobworms, and rarely even any need to dig them out of the ground. Given reasonable conditions – an evening when the moon is clouded over and the air is warm and damp – the worms will come out on to the top of golf courses, cricket pitches and lawns, and you can collect them.

This method of obtaining a supply of lobworms is called 'snitching', but it isn't just a case of wandering around picking up worms. For a start, you must not use a lamp which is too bright, and it is most important to walk along as softly as possible. One clumsy step, and all the worms for yards around will go deep into the ground. On your first snitching expedition, you have to remember that most of the 'lobs' will be anchored into the ground with their tails. After spotting a worm lying on the ground, you have to grab it quietly but quickly – and hold on. Don't pull hard or you will break or damage the worm. Simply hold it firmly until it releases its grip in the ground. Having learnt the art of snitching, it is worthwhile moving from place to place until you find the most wormy piece of grassland in your area. Just half-an-hour in a good worm spot is better than two hours or so in a poor one. If your lobs are to be used within the following two or three days, store them in an airtight bag filled with damp moss. Otherwise, put them in a box or old tub filled with a damp mixture of earth, dead leaves, and grass cuttings. Whether you put them in a bag or box, never include any dead or damaged ones, which could ruin the lot.

As with brandlings and other small red worms, I fish them mostly in halves, size 8 hook being about right. As far as matchmen are concerned, lobworms are most useful in the colder months of the year, especially when the water is coloured after heavy rain. The idea with lob fishing is to cast out and wait, rather than cast here and there every minute or two. I've used lobworms for big chub on the Yorkshire Ouse, and they have provided me with some sizeable bream on the fenland waters in East Anglia. They are also a worthwhile barbel bait, especially on the River Severn. In fact, the largest Severn barbel on record – 12 lb 2 oz – was caught in 1973 by a salmon angler fishing below the weir at Shrewsbury with a bunch of juicy lobs.

20 BREAD

In complete contrast to worms, which are more effective in the colder months from late September onwards, bread baits come more into their own during the balmy days of summer. Not that fish like bream, chub and roach will not eat bread during winter – they often do – but other baits usually offer a better chance on match waters when there is a nip in the air.

Assuming then that you are going to a bream or chub river in summer, bread in one of its various forms should be taken as a priority or standby offering. Breadflake, as it is known in match fishing, is the most simple of bread baits. You just pinch a piece from the middle of a two-day-old white loaf, and nip it on to the bend of a hook. It is important not to allow the hook and flake to dangle in the water prior to casting out, otherwise the bait will not stay the distance. On the other hand, if the flake is still on the hook when you retrieve the tackle, you are nipping it too firmly on the hook. Flake should be 'fluffy' on the outside. When bream are the quarry, I use flake on a number 12 hook, although a bigger piece and a hook of size 8 or 10 will be needed for chub.

Very similar to flake, is bread crust. This is a piece pinched from the outside of a new loaf. You push the point of the hook into the hard crust, and through to the fluffy part underneath. Here again, you should not let the bread become wet before you cast out. Specimen hunters use this on the surface for fish like chub and carp, but I find it a good bait for summer match bream, especially when presented on leger tackle with a swingtip to show bites. Crust is an ideal bream bait at a venue where there is an abundance of weed growth – the River Welland upstream of Crowland Bridge, for example.

Bread paste is one of the oldest angling baits and is still regarded as one of the best. Nevertheless many anglers continue to make paste that is almost useless. They make the big mistake of making it stiff enough to stay on the hook for several casts. And yet, when made properly, it should come off when you strike or reel in quickly. For a start, you need two thick slices from a loaf of white bread two or three days old. Sprinkle some sugar on one of the slices, make a sort of sugar sandwich, and then pour on some boiling water. Let it cool a little, then knead it to a smooth texture. You will probably have to add a few more drops of hot water during the kneading. You can make paste at the waterside with just bread and water, but you will find that the addition of sugar and hot water will make a much more tacky paste. Apart from sugar and water, however, there is no need to add anything else. To ensure that the paste remains at the right consistency, I take it to the waterside in an airtight plastic bag. On the river bank, keep the paste sheltered, where it will not be soaked by rain, or baked by the sun.

On fenland-type waters especially, a most useful bait is groundbait paste, made at the waterside with breadcrumb groundbait and water from the river. Simply put some water in a bowl, add some breadcrumbs (preferably brown, or brown and white mixed) and then mix to a smooth paste, adding bread or water as required. Again, this is a bread bait that should come off the hook when you strike. Groundbait paste is especially effective on bream waters where large amounts of groundbait are thrown in throughout the season. It works particularly well on the lower reaches of the River Welland around Spalding, and also on the hammered River Witham. While I admit to using bread in its various forms mostly to tempt bream these days, there are still chub anglers 'using their loaf' and winning. Come to that, the four-hour match record for the River Wye was set up in 1973 by Monmouthshire angler Arthur Barrett with 79 lb 11 oz of chub to over 6 lb – all on bread! Another water where a large piece of bread on a big hook could prove a winner, is on the famous North Bank stretch of the River Nene downstream of Peterborough, especially as the monster carp there come more into the picture. On the other hand, Trent matchmen rarely find bread worthwhile for any species.

21 CHEESE

On a water where leger tactics frequently produce big and medium-size chub, cheese is always worth a try. Unlike some specimen hunters, though, who don't even mention chub under 5 lb or so, the match angler has to use fairly small pieces of cheese on a moderate size hook, such as a number 10. Besides chub, barbel and roach sometimes fall to an offering of cheese, and this bait can be a winner at any time of the season. Trent chub have a particular liking for cheese, and I wouldn't be surprised if those thriving barbel in that river take a fancy to it.

Whether you use it at the Trent, Yorkshire Ouse, or down on the Thames, the cheese has to be soft. Crumbly stuff is no use at all, and these days I use only soft Cheddar (the kind that comes in square slices for use in sandwiches). It is simply moulded on to a gilt hook, or alternatively you can mix it with soft bread paste. This latter bait is called cheese-paste. When using cheese or cheese-paste on heavily-fished rivers, you often get small knocks before a decisive bite, and it pays to be patient and wait until the fish grab the bait properly.

When waiting for a bite of any kind, you have to be patient. Don't keep reeling in and casting out every few minutes, as this is another of those baits that attracts fish by its smell. It helps if you introduce a few free offerings of cheese into a chub swim now and then. But when cheese is the hookbait, I find it a disadvantage to throw in large balls of cereal groundbait or a lot of maggots and casters. A 4-ounce pack of cheese is normally ample for a match session, even if the fish are 'mad-on'.

A brace of Yorkshire barbel. These powerful fish took luncheon meat

22 LUNCHEON MEAT

Lobworm, bread, cheese and many other things will catch chub and barbel at waters as far apart as the Thames, Severn, and Yorkshire Ouse, but I must admit that my favourite bait for these species is a cube of luncheon meat. In Yorkshire especially, the chub and barbel seem to like this bait more as each year goes by, and they will take it whether the water is low and clear or bank-high and coloured.

The attraction of luncheon meat was proved not long ago when I was asked to catch some fish on the River Swale, in front of cameras, for the B.B.C.'s 'Look North' programme. The filming coincided with the start of the Yorkshire coarse season (June 1st), and as you might expect on such an occasion, there was rubbish coming down in the floodwater, and the Swale was the colour of drinking chocolate. With the very first cast of the day, however, a 4 lb barbel grabbed the bait and was eventually landed. The next try brought only a piece of drifting weed, and then the third cast of the day resulted in another barbel similar to the first. Cameras rolled, the tin of meat bait and the fish were shown to the viewers, and the fishing show was over. The rest of the shoal of barbel had been scared away by the camera crew and the disturbance, but a luncheon meat theory had been well and truly proved.

Luncheon meat catches more fish on leger than if offered on float tackle. I simply cut it into cubes (about $\frac{3}{8}$ inch across) and put it onto a size 10 straight-eyed gilt hook. Now and then it pays to introduce just three or four pieces of meat into the swim, but I never overdo the free offerings, and rarely use more than one small tin in one outing. Some matchmen make a paste of luncheon meat and bread, but I have never found this to give an advantage and to be better than meat on its own. I also advise against using really large lumps of meat on big hooks in matches. That way is all right for a man who can wait days for one specimen fish, but in contests we can't afford to let those $1\frac{1}{2}$ lb, 2 lb and 3 lb chub and barbel pass us by.

A final tip for luncheon-meat users. Some meat sinks and some floats, so find a brand which goes to the bottom when cut into cubes. If you have floating meat, you will not be able to give the chub and barbel a few 'free' pieces.

23 HEMPSEED AND TARES

Hempseed is usually sold as bird food, is a small black seed of the hemp plant, and is mostly grown in Chile. In contrast, tares are the dark-coloured seed of a weed that grows among corn in this country. They are slightly larger than hempseed, and are sold as cattle fodder and pigeon food. Each of these baits has to be cooked in water before use.

One of the best things that has ever happened in match fishing, was when the National Federation of Anglers lifted their match ban on hempseed. This is a most deadly roach bait, and it can be used to encourage big fish of all species to come on feed, even if you are using something altogether different on the hook. Many match anglers at the Witham these days, for instance, put some grains of hemp in the bread groundbait, even if they are hoping to catch the bream on maggot, worms, and caster. It is a similar story at the River Trent where roach anglers are introducing hempseed and casters, and baiting the hook with caster. When doing this cross-baiting, you don't usually catch more fish, but it certainly brings a bigger share of sizeable ones.

Used on its own as free offerings and hookbait, hemp often has no equal, and in recent years Trent experts such as Newark's Barrie Wright and George Robinson have taken top prizes with it. When using hemp, it pays to tackle up with a size 18 hook (or a size 16 if the hemp is larger than average). My way is to push the bend of the hook into the seed, leaving the point of the hook just showing. Don't make the frequent mistake of using too much hempseed and overfeeding the fish. A cupful would be ample on an average match outing, although you could double that amount if the fish were exceptionally ravenous. It is easy to prepare; simply empty it into a saucepan, cover with water, then bring to the boil and simmer until the white kernels of the seed start to show. The cooking period takes less than an hour. Keep it damp until you are ready to use it. To make sure it is fresh, I always cook it the evening before a contest.

The latest trend among hempseed anglers is to carry on feeding the swim with hempseed, but to use a tare on the hook. There are two advantages when using tare – you can use a bigger hook (a number 14) and it tends to sort out a larger class of roach. It also helps, I think, if you feed the swim with tares as well as hempseed. In fact, some of the top roach anglers use tares on their own without any hempseed at all. My preference is to use both. On the River Witham especially, this hemp and tare combination can be really deadly in summer. It is a summer-only way of fishing, however, and I wouldn't bother with tares at all in icy weather, unless the river was artificially warmed by a nearby power station.

The preparation of tares is a slow job. You have to cook them until they become fairly soft, but at the same time you have to make sure that the dark-coloured outer skins remain intact. You will never need more than one cupful of tares for one match. While hempseed and tares will take fish at all depths, it certainly pays to lay on or trail the bottom. This way – as opposed to fishing these baits in midwater – you get better bites and better fish.

A final tip for tare anglers – never try to bury the hook, otherwise you will miss more bites than you hit.

24 WASP GRUB

In recent years, wasp grub has caused more controversy than all the other baits put together. In fact a number of clubs have banned the use of this deadly bait altogether. The men against wasp grubs argue – rightly or wrongly – that not everyone has the time to collect enough for a big match. It is true that some men in summer actually do spend more time seeking wasp grubs than they do catching fish. Some competitors on chub rivers think nothing of taking five or six complete nests. Whether or not this bait should be permitted is for individual clubs and associations to decide, but if it is allowed on your chubby stretch of match river, there is no alternative but to get out and 'follow that wasp'.

Following the route of wasps is the best way to find a nest. Watch the wasps flying by, go the same way as those that are taking a straight path, and you should end up at the nest. Whatever you do, don't go too near at this stage. Usually, the nest is built in a hole in the ground, and there are always many angry wasps coming and going during the daytime, especially in the warm sunny weather. It is best to return to the nest towards dusk, when most of the 'tenants' will be indoors for the night. This way, there is less chance of you getting stung.

The next step is to sprinkle a quantity of chemical insect killer in the mouth of the nest. Chub and pike expert Ray Webb has used a substance containing cyanide for many years, boiling it in water and then scattering it inside the entrance of the nest. However, I wouldn't do it that way, as it is too dangerous. It is much safer to use a proprietary brand of insect killer which can be purchased without having to sign a 'poisons' book at the chemists. Some anglers use carbon tetrachloride, and although slow to kill wasps, it is fairly safe. In any case, you should be able to return a day later and dig out the lovely grubs. By the way, if the nest is on rough ground, it will pay to stick a pole or something in the ground to act as a marker. Otherwise you may kill the wasps all right, but not be able to find the nest on the following day.

After digging out the nest, separate a good number for use as hookbait. Then the rest of the grubs and the cake are scalded with water, mashed into a pulp, and mixed with fine breadcrumbs. This wasp-nest mash will be your groundbait for use when some grubs are on the hook. If you are not using the nest or nests straight away, or are building up a stock for the winter, put the complete cakes in airtight plastic bags and keep in a deep freeze.

Armed with a nest or two for a chub session, I think that the best hook sizes are numbers 10 and 12. You can fish wasp grubs singly, but I much prefer to offer three or four at a time. With wasp grubs being so soft and fragile, some may come off the hook anyway. Obviously, it pays to swing the tackle out rather than give it a jerk. In contrast to luncheon meat, which I prefer to fish on leger tackle, wasp grub accounts for more fish when it is presented on the move on a float rig. On the type of river where wasp grub works best – like the Severn or Yorkshire Ouse – you will need a fair-sized float and a number of big shot to allow you to fish it properly.

I have pointed out that, on average, float tackle is the best way to present wasp grubs, and that the grub is mainly a chub bait, but in our world of angling there are always exceptions to the rule. Only a few years ago, for instance, Yorkshire match angler James O'Brien won a club match on the Yorkshire Ouse with a fabulous haul of 82 lb 15 oz. Those fish took grubs legered on swingtip tackle – and they were barbel!

Bloodworms

25 BLOODWORMS

Bloodworms are not worms as we usually know them at all, in fact they are a midge larva and live on the bottom of stagnant pools. The water doesn't have to be clean and pure or anything like that. In fact, my favourite bloodworm spot is fairly smelly. This is just one reason why bloodworms are not as popular as some other baits. It is also true that bloodworms often attract tiny fish, and I've caught hundreds of sticklebacks on this bait while trying for roach and perch. On the credit side, though, they are useful on waters like some of those in Lancashire where a pound or two of fish can often win.

The first time I was introduced to bloodworm fishing was at Wigan. And I'll tell you, if anybody knows anything about bloodworms, it is those small-hook and fine-line specialists of Wigan. It is a horrible business collecting bloodworms, I can assure you. Most of the time you are up to or over your knees in mud and water. The Wigan way, is to use a thin strip of metal fastened onto the end of a broomstick. You slice the blade through the mud in the bottom, and – if you have hit on a good spot – there should be a number of tiny red worms draped over the edge at every scoop. The bloodworms (which will be a bit muddy) are all put into a nylon stocking and given a good rinse. After that, keep them in damp peat in newspaper. English bloodworm experts mostly offer them on hook sizes of 20 and 22. By our standards, those hooks are exceptionally small, yet in France and Belgium, they often use bloodworm on hooks as tiny as 26 and 28. To speed things up and save time on re-baiting, continentals often use a bloodworm substitute called 'Mystic' on the hook. It is a bright red substance that can easily be shaped to look like a tiny worm, and it is now available in this country. By the way, a bloodworm has a stubby head at one end and a forked tail at the other. The hook is inserted towards the head.

Anyway, that is the way to use bloodworms, and I am sure they will continue to win cups and money on hard waters. They are not among my favourite baits, however, and I feel it is a pity that there are waters poor enough to call for their use.

26 CEREAL GROUNDBAIT

The basic ingredient of my groundbait these days is breadcrumb. You can buy it fine, medium, coarse, brown or white. My way is to get a quantity of medium grade white crumbs and mix with an equal amount of medium grade brown crumbs. This produces a groundbait mixture that can be wetted to almost any consistency. In the old days, I used to make my own by leaving left-over crusts in an oven overnight, and then spend hours carefully putting it through a mincer. I don't do it that way these days. In fact, if I still did – considering the amount I use in a season – I would be doing nothing but fish and make groundbait!

The best way is to collect some groundbait from your tackle dealer, a few weeks before the mad rush for bait and tackle at the start of the match season. It may even pay you to place an order with your tackle man weeks in advance, as I do. It pays, too, to buy groundbait in bags of half-hundredweight or one hundredweight. I prefer the smaller of these two, if only because it is easier to handle. I have a bag of white and a bag of brown, and put an equal quantity of each into my canvas bait carrier. By collecting bait in fairly large quantities, it works out much cheaper than buying a small bag before every trip. To make sure that the breadcrumbs do not become lumpy or mouldy during storage, it is important to keep the crumbs in a dry place. Whatever you do, don't ever take mouldy bread to a contest, or it could do a lot more harm than good.

Armed with a canvas bag holding anything between 1 and 1½ stone of brown and white bait, the next thing is to decide on the type of bait required – cloud (the type you would use for roach on a stillwater); a normal bream mix (like you would use to take squats, gozzers, and casters to a far off spot on a river like the Witham, Great Ouse or Huntspill); and really heavy stuff that is only used in a very strong flow. Whichever type is called for, you need a wide shallow bowl, and it is best to put some water (from the river) in first, followed by the necessary amount of bait. For cloud, hardly any water at all is required, while the really heavy stuff will need to soak up quite a lot. When a heavy mix is wanted, I find it is best to mix it a bit too wet, allow it to soak for a few minutes, then add dry bait until you get it just right. To test whether a bait is firm enough to withstand a long throw, I sometimes make a ball before the start of a match, and lob it into the field behind me. Remember, though, the more things like squats, pinkies and maggots you put in the mix, the more likely it is to break up in mid-air. Incidentally, forget all those silly ideas about mixing bait with water at home and then carrying it wet to the waterside. I find I've enough weight to carry anyway, and I'm also sure that a fresh mix is usually a better texture.

As far as additives to bread groundbait are concerned, I advise you to forget all those fairy tales of magic chemicals. On the other hand, if I am taking bleak and roach on the drop, I would add a handful or two of dry maize meal. This makes the mix really light, and is the only thing I would put in cloud. Some old anglers add semolina to lighten bread bait, but maize does the job much better and improves the colour.

When a heavy mix is called for (and I really do mean heavy), you can find it an advantage to add a few big handfuls of yellow rusk. This really stiffens things. In fact, if you got a combination of bread and yellow rusk just right, I reckon it would make an ideal material for a garden path!

Bran can make bread bait more acceptable to bream, but it is a thing that must be kept well away from the home. Very often, bran is full of tiny mites, and – unless you are careful – they get everywhere. If you use it at all, take care to wash out the bait bowl after every trip, and make sure to give the inside of the basket a regular sprinkle with insecticide powder. Years ago, I once discovered that all my reels, hooks and floats (and even the rod butts) were covered with the blessed things, and it was several weeks before I discovered that a bag of bran was the source of the trouble. Sorry if I have made you scratch, but I had to warn you. Who knows? You may have them already!

One thing I have been experimenting with in groundbait is black silt. Apart from the tiny living things it may contain, I feel a darker bait is less likely to alarm fish, especially when the water is gin clear. Certainly, whenever I am adding chopped worms to bait, I always include the black peat in which they have been stored. In fact, some of the Lancashire bloodworm experts use black peat and leafmould, and no bread at all. Whatever you put or don't put in your bait, you have to be careful how much you use. I have taken a couple of stone in summer and used it to advantage in a swim full of ravenous bream. And yet, in winter especially, a couple of handfuls can be too much if there are only a few lethargic fish around. Very often it is a case of trial and error, and if for instance, you find that the use of groundbait slows bites up, you should keep your hand out of the bowl. On the other hand, it sometimes brings more fish than ever. The fish will decide which way is right and which way is wrong.

27 SANDWICH BAITS

Fish are very much like humans, and they can't always make up their minds about what sort of food they want to eat. This, I think, is the main reason why so-called sandwich baits have become increasingly popular on the match scene in recent years. Often when there is more than one kind of bait on one hook, it is referred to as a cocktail. Call them sandwich or cocktail, but I can assure you the idea is worthwhile, especially in the colder months when fish are hard to tempt and one or two big ones can be enough for top prize.

The most common is a worm and maggot cocktail. I simply put on half a worm first, then follow with one or two white or yellow maggots. More recently, worm and caster have proved successful for bream, and this works particularly well if you are putting chopped worms and casters in the cereal groundbait. Some match anglers swear by an offering of maggot and caster on the same hook, although I must admit that this idea has never proved rewarding for me. Mind you, I have a lot of faith in maggots of mixed colours together, and I have also done well with bream when using double maggot tipped with a pinkie or a couple of squats.

My favourite sandwich bait of all – and it is something

that has not yet caught on with matchmen – is a cube of luncheon meat and two maggots. This mixed offering is deadly for barbel, as I proved on a recent outing with the editor of my local angling newspaper. He had never caught a Yorkshire Ouse barbel, but I rigged him up with a meat and maggot cocktail at Nun Monkton, and in next to no time he was fighting it out with a 4¾-pounder. You may think it was one of those things, but this kind of thing with meat and maggots has happened too many times to be a fluke. When using this barbel cocktail, I free offer with maggots only. I think the barbel move upstream mopping up maggots, then regard themselves lucky if they find a pair of maggots, and also a tasty bonus of meat. Whatever the reason, they certainly take it with a bang.

Part Three

FUTURE TRENDS

In match angling it is often said that it takes at least ten years for a new idea really to catch on and become accepted as a winning method. Nevertheless, ways with tackle and baits are gradually changing all the time, and the ambitious matchman must always keep in step with any new trends that could improve his chances of success.

Average match-winning weights of today are much higher than they were forty and fifty years ago, and this is in spite of water pollution and bigger numbers of anglers on the river banks. This improvement in sport is likely to continue, but only for those who think deeply about methods and use only the best tackle and baits available.

It seems certain that any future improvements in winning match catches will come about because of better bait and presentation, rather than because of improved methods of bite detection. Floats, swingtips and quivertips have been developed to a stage where there is little room for improvement. Yet I am sure the top match anglers of the next few decades will discover even more successful baits and better terminal tackles. In all fishing, the main thing is first to get the fish to give a good bite, and most of the future trends will certainly be in this direction.

In this book, I have introduced you to all the winning equipment and baits. At the same time, however, never forget that there is no substitute for practice sessions at the waterside. And while for instance you may have the best float and baits on a particular match water, they are unlikely to bring a top prize if you are not familiar with them.

MATCH FISHING TERMS

AAA A size of lead shot, approximately 30 to the ounce and just over $\frac{3}{16}$ inch in diameter.

ANATTO This is used to make maggots a butter colour. It is added to feed when maggots are being bred. Anattoes are maggots coloured by this method.

ANTENNA A popular type of match float, which is most useful in windy conditions. It has a long cane stem at the top and a body of balsa at the bottom.

ARLESEY BOMBS These are streamlined leger weights with a swivel moulded in at one end. For match fishing, the most useful sizes are $\frac{1}{4}$, $\frac{3}{8}$, $\frac{1}{2}$ and $\frac{3}{4}$ ounce.

BACKING This is used partly to fill a deep reel spool, prior to the nylon line being wound on. It is not necessary on a shallow match spool.

BACK SHOTTING This is when lead shot is put on the line above the float. It can be used to sink line in windy conditions.

BAIT DROPPER A small bait container which opens and releases the free offerings when it hits the river bed.

BAIT STAND A series of clips that can be screwed onto the top of a bank stick. Maggot cartons can then be clipped on and positioned near to hand.

BALE ARM The part of a fixed-spool reel that folds over and picks up the line so that it can be reeled in.

BANK STICK A piece of tubular steel, pointed at one end and threaded at the other. Used for holding a rod rest or keepnet. Sizes range between 2 and 4 feet in length.

BARB A projection just below the point of a hook; when a fish is hooked, it helps keep the hook embedded.

BARBLESS A hook with no barb. Useful for high-speed bleak fishing.

BATTING A method for reeling in quickly with a centre pin reel. The angler hits the drum of the reel to make it revolve.

BB A size of lead shot, approximately $\frac{5}{32}$ inch in diameter.

BITE When a fish takes a baited hook. Usually indicated by the movement of a float, swingtip or quiver-tip.

BLOODWORM A small bright red worm found at the bottom of stagnant pools. Used by matchmen on waters where small fish offer a winning chance.

BLOWS The eggs laid by a bluebottle or similar fly. After a few days they become tiny maggots.

BOMB Short for Arlesey bomb.

BOMB LINK A link of nylon line fastened or sliding on the reel line above the hook, and having a leger weight or a string of shots fastened on the other end.

BRANDLING A small red worm with yellow rings around its body. It is often found in pig manure heaps, and is a good winter match bait, especially for bream.

BREAKING STRAIN The weight a fishing line will lift.

BUTT The bottom section of a fishing rod, usually covered with a cork handle.

BUTT INDICATOR A bite indicator that clips onto the butt section of a rod.

BUTT LOADING Weight inserted into the bottom of a rod butt to make the rod more balanced.

BUTT RING The rod ring nearest to the cork handle – usually fitted with a hard jewel insert.

CAPTA A pyramid-shaped leger weight, fitted with a swivel.

CASTERS A name given to a maggot when it has become a chrysalis. It is when they are light red in colour and sink below the surface that they are most useful.

CENTRE PIN A drum-type reel, with the spool part revolving on a pin. They are usually made of light alloy.

CHRYSODINE A dye that can be used to colour maggots a yellow-orange.

CLOSED FACE A type of fixed-spool reel with line pick-up and spool enclosed.

CLOSE SEASON A rest period for fish when no angling is allowed.

CLOUD BAIT A fine cereal groundbait, usually fine breadcrumbs, rusk or maize meal.

COCKIES Another name for ruffe. Used by many northern match anglers, especially around Leeds and York.

COFFIN LEGER These leger weights are almost rectangular in shape, similar to a coffin. They are best if fished on a sliding link of nylon line.

CRYSTAL A pattern of hook that has a fairly sharp bend above the point. Especially good when maggot is the hook bait.

DISGORGER A thin metal tool for removing a hook from inside the mouth of a fish. Not suitable for big spade end or eyed hooks.

DISPENSER A circular box which holds several different sizes of lead shot in separate compartments.

DOUBLE DRAW When a match angler draws more than one peg number. Not usually permitted.

DOUBLE PEGGED When a river is numbered for a match along opposite banks.

DOUBLE RUBBER When a float is secured on the line

at both ends by means of small pieces of plastic or rubber tube.

DRAG Short for weed drag. Used for clearing away troublesome weed.

DRAW When match anglers draw a number out of a bag (a draw bag). They then have to fish at that number on the river bank.

DUST SHOTS The smallest sizes of lead shot, numbers 6, 7 and 8.

END RING The jewelled rod ring on the thin top part of a rod.

EYED HOOK A hook with an eye on the end of the shank. These are usually tied directly on to the reel line.

FEEDER A half-grown maggot. Rarely used these days, as squats and pinkies are much preferred.

FIXED-SPOOL A popular type of fishing reel. The spool does not revolve, the line is wound on to it by the pick-up or bale-arm mechanism.

FLAKE A piece of bread pinched from the inside of a loaf.

FLOAT CAPS Coloured plastic covers that fit onto the top of floats. An angler can choose a colour to suit the prevailing conditions.

FLOAT RUBBERS Short pieces of rubber or plastic tube for holding the float in position on the line.

FOUL HOOKED This is when a fish is accidentally hooked on its tail or fins, not in its mouth.

FREE OFFERINGS Small amounts of hook bait thrown into the water to encourage fish to start feeding.

GILT CRYSTAL A gold-plated crystal bend hook.

GOZZER A maggot bred from the carcase of a wood pigeon. They are mostly used for bream, and are softer than ordinary maggots.

GROOVING When rod rings are worn by the line.

GROUNDBAIT This name is given to any form of free offering, but in match fishing it means a cereal mixture such as breadcrumbs or rusk.

GRUB Short for wasp grub. Used for chub, especially on waters like the River Severn and Yorkshire Ouse.

HALF BLOOD A knot used for joining the end of a nylon line onto a loop of nylon.

HEMPSEED A small black seed bait used mainly for roach.

HOLDING BACK When a float is steadied in a river, so that the bait precedes it downstream.

HUSK A northern name for maggot chrysalis.

IDLE-BACK A Yorkshire name for a rod rest.

JEWELLED RUNNER A butt or end ring lined with a hard-wearing material.

LAYING-ON A float fishing method, with the baited hook laid on the river bed.

LEGERING Fishing with the bait on the river bed, anchored in position with a leger weight. Usually no float is used, and bites are indicated by a swingtip, quiver-tip or rod tip.

LEGER WEIGHT A piece of lead such as an Arlesey bomb or pear lead, or a string of swan shots.

LEFT BANK The left-hand bank of a river facing downstream.

LIFT BITE A bite that is indicated by a lift of the float.

LINE BITE This is caused when a fish swims into the line and gives a false bite.

LIVERS Maggots bred on cow, sheep or pig liver.

LOBS Abbreviation of lobworm. These big worms can be collected on lawns and golf courses after dark. A good bait for chub and barbel.

MAGGOT The larva of a bluebottle, usually obtainable at tackle shops.

MAGGOT BAG A cloth maggot container which is hung around the angler's neck.

MAGGOT PIES Hollow balls of mud or groundbait filled with maggots.

MATCH STRETCH Part of a river being used for a contest.

MCKENZIE A pattern of hook with a round bend. A good shape for use with casters.

N.A.C. Abbreviation of National Anglers' Council, a body formed to further the interests of all anglers.

NATIONAL CHAMPIONSHIPS Major contests organised by the National Federation of Anglers. Formerly known as the 'All England'.

N.F.A. Abbreviation of National Federation of Anglers.

NYLON MONOFILAMENT A single strand of nylon fishing line.

OPEN MATCH A match anyone can join.

PATERNOSTER A leger tackle rig with the lead on the bottom and the hook and bait held above it at any desired depth.

PEACOCK A float made of peacock quill.

PEAR A pear-shaped leger weight.

PEGGED OUT When a river has been numbered ready for a match.

PEGGER A man who puts numbers along a river bank.

PEG LEG When a float is fastened on the line at the bottom end only (opposite to double rubber).

PEGS Numbers on the bank of a match stretch.

PICK UP Another name for bale arm.

PIMPING A type of match fishing when the aim is a net full of tiny fish. A man who fishes this way is sometimes referred to as a pimper.

PINKIE A small maggot, the larva of the greenbottle.

PINKS Another name for minnow. This tiny fish is often a nuisance to the match angler.

PLUMMET A bomb-shaped piece of lead which is used for plumbing the depth of water.

PORKY Abbreviation of porcupine. A streamlined float made from the quill of a porcupine.

PUMPING A way of bringing a fish in without putting too much strain on the reel. The rod is lifted, then while reeling in, the rod tip is lowered. The rod is lifted again, and the process is repeated until the fish is in the landing net.

QUIVER-TIP A thin piece of fibre-glass that screws into the top runner of a rod, and indicates bites on leger tackle.

RIGHT BANK The right-hand side of a river facing downstream.

ROACH POLE A rod with no rings on, used widely on the Continent. The line is connected to the top of the rod, and no reel is necessary.

ROD REST A rest for putting the rod on while legering, baiting the hook, or unhooking fish.

ROD RING The rings on a rod through which the line runs freely.

RUFFE A tiny fish of the perch family.

RUNNERS Another name for rod rings.

SANDWICH BAITS Two or more types of bait on the same hook.

SARKANDAS A reed from which float stems are made.

SELF COCKERS Floats that stand up in the water without any lead shot on the line. They have a limited range of uses.

SHOP A fishing spot you have been allotted in a contest. This term is used a lot in the Nottingham area.

SHORT DRAW A length of nylon line only 12 or 18 inches long with a hook fastened on the end.

SHOT BITES False bites sometimes encountered when hempseed fishing. The fish bite the lead shot instead of the hemp.

SIZE LIMITS The minimum size that fish can be retained in keepnets or killed.

SKIMMER A name given to an awkward downstream wind, and also to small bream.

SLACK Part of a river where there is no flow.

SLIDER Another name for sliding float – a float that allows you to fish deep water. It slides on the line and is stopped by a cotton or nylon knot.

SLIPPING CLUTCH The part of a reel that can be adjusted to prevent line breakage.

SNITCHING The art of collecting lobworms on lawns and fields after dark.

SPADE END A type of hook with the end of the shank flattened. Becoming more popular than ever.

SPOOL The part of a reel on which the line is wound.

SQUATS These tiny maggots are the larvae of the common housefly.

STAKER Another name for pegger.

STICK FLOAT A tapered float made of balsa and cane or balsa and wire.

STOPPER A cork plug for protecting the female part of a rod ferrule.

STRAY A fish on its own away from the shoal.

STRET PEGGING A method of float fishing on a flowing water. A form of laying-on.

STRIKE The act of setting the hook after a fish has taken the bait.

SWAN A size of lead shot, 15 to the ounce, and just over $\frac{1}{4}$ inch in diameter. Sometimes called SSG shot.

SWIM The part of a river from one peg number to the next one downstream.

SWIM FEEDER A small container that is packed with maggots, casters or any other bait. It is fastened onto a leger rig, and is used to put some free samples of food near the hook bait.

SWIMMING DOWN Allowing float tackle to drift downstream with the current.

SWINGTIP A bite indicator which hangs from the rod tip. It is made of nylon or cane.

SWIVEL A small metal link which prevents the line becoming twisted.

TAIL The distance between the bomb link and the hook; or between the bottom shot and the hook.

TARES A fairly small dark seed, which is an excellent summer roach bait.

TARGET BOARD A marked board which helps bite detection when using swingtip tackle.

TERMINAL TACKLE All the tackle on the end of the line – hook, float, shots and leger weight.

THROWING STICK This is used for sending bait to the far side of a river. A hollow piece of cane or fibre-glass, plugged about 2 inches from one end.

TOMMY RUFFE Another name for ruffe, a tiny fish of the perch family.

TOP PART The thin top section of a rod.

TROTTING DOWN Another name for swimming down.

WAGGLER A peacock-stemmed float, with a balsa body at the bottom.

WATERLICKED When an angler has caught nothing.

WEIGHER A man who weighs the catches at the finish of a match.

WHIPPING Cotton or silk thread used to fasten the rings on a rod.

WHITE BREAM A name given to a silver bream or any small bream.

WILLOW BLADE A northern name for bleak, a small surface-feeding fish.

WINCH FITTINGS Used for securing a reel to the handle of a rod.

WINTER LEAGUES Team competitions staged in the colder months of the year.

YARD BOTTOM This is a yard of nylon line with a hook on the end.

ZANDER Often referred to as pike-perch, and are a common species in the Great Ouse river system.

ZOOMER An antenna-type float loaded with lead at the bottom.